Appliqué
The basics and beyond

by Janet Pittman

Landauer Books

Appliqué
The basics and beyond
by Janet Pittman

This book was designed, produced, and published by Landauer Books
A division of Landauer Corporation
3100 NW 101st Street, Urbandale, IA 50322
800-557-2144; www.landauercorp.com

President/Publisher: Jeramy Lanigan Landauer
Editor-in-Chief: Becky Johnston
Art Director: Lyne Neymeyer
Illustrations: Janet Pittman
Technical Editor: Kristine Peterson
Technical Assistants: Mary V. Cecil, Patty Barrett
Photography: Dean Tanner—Primary Image Ltd.

Library of Congress Cataloging-in-Publication Data
Pittman, Janet
   Appliqué : the basics and beyond : the complete guide to successful machine and hand techniques with dozens of designs to mix and match / by Janet Pitttman.
      p. cm.
ISBN-13: 978-1-890621-06-3 (alk. paper)
ISBN-10: 1-890621-06-4 (alk. paper)
1. Appliqué. 2. Quilting. I. Title.
TT779.P57 2006
746.44'5--dc22   2006045267
This book is printed on acid-free paper.
Printed in China
10 9 8 7 6 5 4 3

ISBN 13: 978-1-890621-06-3

On the front cover: The four quadrants of Bearded Iris were prepared and stitched using the following techniques: **(upper left)** invisible machine appliqué embellished by hand with back stitches; **(upper right)** fusible-web appliqué embellished by machine with programmed satin stitches: **(lower left)** fusible-web appliqué embellished by machine with free-motion zigzag stitches; and **(lower right)** hand appliqué embellished by hand with French knots and long stitches.

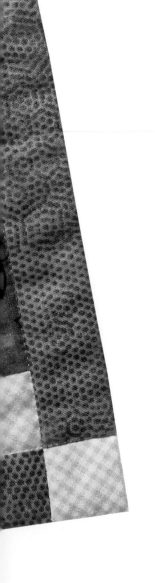

where to find it

getting started—basics and beyond

You'll find all the basics of machine and hand appliqué, along with my special techniques for machine embellishing in the following chapters: Equipment & Supplies, Preparing Appliqué, Stitching, and Embellishing. Each chapter is presented in an easy-to-follow format. I've designed seven Projects, each with specific steps on stitching and embellishing. Be inspired by the projects and then treat yourself to full-size patterns plus options for designing your own unique appliqué quilts. *Janet*

Equipment & Supplies is a must first read. Use this information for selecting tools and supplies as you prepare appliqué pieces and stitch appliqué projects. Most of the equipment and supplies will be familiar to experienced needle workers. Experiment with the unfamiliar to ease the appliqué process and enhance your work.

Preparing Appliqué explains how to make appliqué pieces for fusible-web appliqué, invisible machine appliqué, other machine appliqué techniques, and hand appliqué. Detailed instructions and photographs are given for each preparation technique. Review the various techniques and practice them with a simple leaf or heart pattern to discover your preference.

- Fusible-web appliqué is quick and easy to use for intricate shapes.
- Invisible machine appliqué has the look of hand appliqué.
- Hand appliqué is more traditional, but is portable, and many needle workers find it to be relaxing.
- Turned edges result in a more classic look and can be machine- or hand-stitched.

Stitching demonstrates the many machine utility stitches and basic hand stitches used for appliqué. Each stitch type example gives details of when to use the stitch, how to set up the machine for stitching, and special stitching instructions. Illustrations show corner and curve techniques. An actual-size photograph shows both stitching in red thread to emphasize the stitch pattern and stitching with a typical thread that might be used on a project.

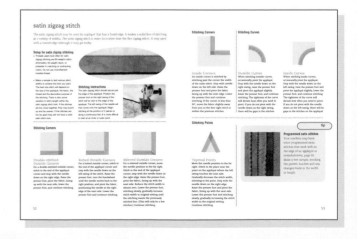

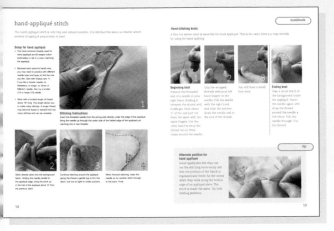

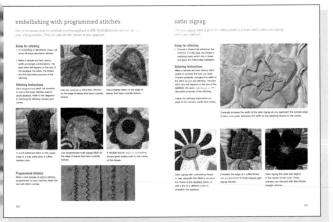

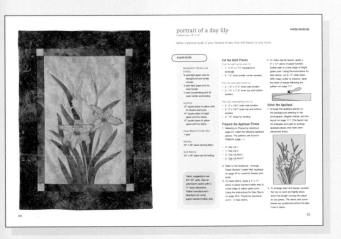

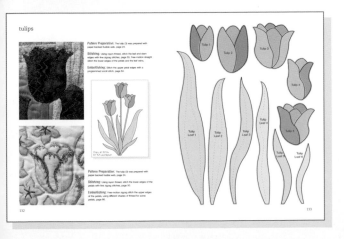

Notebook includes sections of information that are important to many of the techniques in a chapter. The yellow background alerts you to review the information.

Tips offer helpful ideas for making your appliqué better or easier. They are not essential to the process, but are easy to identify with a green or blue background.

Embellishing describes many stitches, both machine and hand, that can be used to give your appliqué texture and definition. Embellishing is used to emphasize or enhance the appliqué design. Sometimes an embellishing stitch is used on the edge of an appliqué piece instead of a utility stitch. Beading embellishments are attached after layering. In addition to technical how-to steps, this chapter shows many uses of embellishing in projects. Practicing the embellishing techniques will make them part of your needlework repertoire.

Projects showcases seven appliqué quilts. The level of difficulty ranges from basic (the small Clematis Treasure with a single flower), to advanced (the intricate Spring Border) sure to challenge your appliqué skills. For each project there are detailed stitching and embellishing instructions. The **Be Creative** section included at the end of most projects features variations for using the background with other patterns in the book. A unique project can be created by mixing and matching patterns, stitches, and embellishments using the techniques presented in other chapters. To easily identify this section, look for the seafoam green background.

Patterns includes all the patterns to make the projects in this book, as well as many options. Some of these options will be types or sizes of patterns which may be best for hand appliqué, turned-edge appliqué, or fusible-web appliqué. The pattern pages also include close-up photographs of stitching and embellishing options and a sample layout for using the patterns.

making a project—basics and beyond

When you are familiar with the appliqué techniques in this book, choose a project you'd like to make. I suggest using the design as a starting point, and then change the elements as desired to create your own unique Spring Border.

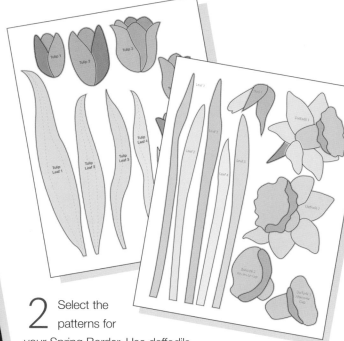

2 Select the patterns for your Spring Border. Use daffodils, tulips, narcissus, and muscari, or use one of the variations or another flower and leaf combination to place on the prepared fence background.

1 Select the project you'd like to make.

3 Select your appliqué technique and pattern preparation method. You may make the project as presented using paper-backed fusible web techniques or choose your favorite preparation and stitching methods. For example, the daffodils have an optional cup pattern that would be easier to use for invisible machine stitching or hand appliqué.

4 Select colors and textures for your project. If you want the flowers to be realistically colored and embellished, take some time for a little research. Refer to plant catalogs, garden magazines, snap shots, and real flowers to get ideas.

steps to success

Select:
1 project
2 patterns
3 method of appliqué
4 colors and textures
5 fabrics
6 arrangement
7 stitches
8 embellishments

5 Select your fabrics and try out the colors next to each other. Here are several possible fence fabrics shown against the sky fabric.

6 Try different flower arrangements and colors after the background and fence are stitched. First, prepare the flower unit motifs, page 44. Arrange the flowers and foliage, referring to the illustrated layout or as desired. Overlapping some leaves and stems gives the design depth. Remember, if you are simulating nature, no two flowers grow alike. Fuse the flowers and foliage to the background.

7 Practice stitching and embellishing, following the suggestions in the project and using the techniques featured on each pattern page and in *Stitching* and *Embellishing*. Stitch the edges.

8 Add the borders, layer, quilt, and bind your project. Embellish the flower centers with beads and add hand couching or embroidery.

9

equipment
& supplies

Discover how easy
it is to get started
in machine and
hand appliqué by
adding a few unique items to the
basic equipment and supplies
that you may already have on
hand for patchwork quilting.

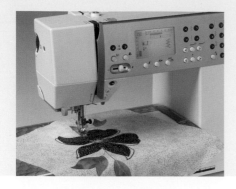

equipment & supplies

After reviewing this information and the techniques in the next few chapters, check with quilting friends who machine or hand appliqué. Find out about their favorite techniques. Decide what you would like to practice, and purchase the best equipment and supplies you can.

Sewing Machine Features

For machine appliqué, a sewing machine with zigzag capabilities is a must. The best machine to use will have the needed features and will work with you rather than give you problems. Clean your machine of lint, oil it regularly, and have it serviced as recommended by the manufacturer.

For machine appliqué look for the following sewing machine features:

Bobbin Case

An adjustable lower bobbin tension. If you have a removable bobbin case you may want to purchase a second one just for adjusting for differing thread weights and a variety of stitches. Mark this bobbin "for machine appliqué only."

Top Tension

An adjustable upper thread tension for making even stitches when using different weights of thread.

Stitch Width and Length

An adjustable stitch length and width allowing you to make decorative choices in your zigzag stitches, blanket stitch, and decorative appliqué stitches. A stitch width with enough adjusting points to allow for a smooth transition from wide to narrow and back will allow you to control points and to do decorative satin stitching.

Needle Position

An adjustable needle position feature allowing you to find the best combination of needle position and presser foot for guiding your stitching.

It is helpful to have a needle up/needle down function. Leaving the needle down at the end of a stitch allows you to pivot your work without it slipping out of place.

Feed Dogs

Feed dogs which can be lowered allow for a smooth transition to free-motion stitching. Some machines have a plate to cover the feed dogs, and you will have to remove your work to add the plate.

Feed Dogs Up

Feed Dogs Down

Speed Adjustment

A speed adjustment option is useful when doing stitching such as satin zigzag or free-motion zigzag where there is a wide swing of the needle, close stitching, or for top stitching.

Throat Plate

If your machine has an extra-wide throat plate (9mm), purchase a narrower (5mm) throat plate for fine and narrow zigzag stitching. You will need extra stabilizing, page 49, with extra-wide zigzag stitching.

Presser Feet

Most machines come with a selection of presser feet. The presser feet shown here are especially useful for machine appliqué. If you do not have them, consider purchasing them.

Open-Toe Embroidery or Appliqué Foot with Grooved Bottom

An open-toe embroidery or appliqué foot features a wide opening in front so you can see the stitching. It also has a groove molded in the bottom to allow the build up of thread from stitching to pass under it smoothly.

Edge-Stitch Foot

The edge-stitching foot has a metal flange that moves along the edge of the appliqué allowing straight stitches and blanket stitches to be sewn more accurately.

Darning Feet

A darning foot which allows the free moving of material under the foot is necessary for free-motion straight and zigzag stitching. This is the same foot you use for free-motion quilting. Two varieties are shown here.

Walking Foot

A walking foot is designed to move the upper fabric the same as the feed dogs move the bottom fabric. Use when straight stitching turned-edge appliqué and when stitching and quilting in one step after layering.

Machine Needles

Machine needles come in a variety of sizes, designs, and quality. Purchase the best quality needles and replace as necessary.

Machine needles are manufactured for specific jobs, and their names are an indication of that. Needles vary in sharpness of the point, size of the eye, and thickness of the blade. Select the smallest needle with the appropriate eye and blade for your project.

The size of the needle is frequently marked in both European and U. S. numbers. The European numbers start at 60 and the U. S. numbers start at 8. You will frequently see a size marked as 60/8. Both numbers get larger as the needle gets larger.

The other differences in machine needles are the point and the eye. These are marked by letters. H-M has the sharpest point and can be used for straight and zigzag stitching on cotton and silk with cotton or silk thread. H-E is an embroidery needle which has a larger eye and specially designed groove for decorative threads. 130/MET is designed with a finish to help control the heat from friction when stitching with metallic threads. It also has a special eye to prevent splitting of metallic threads. 130/N is designed with a special eye to accommodate heavy threads.

equipment & supplies

Hand-Stitching Needles

Hand-stitching needles are available in a variety of sizes, lengths, designs, and quality. Purchase the best quality needles and replace as they become dull or bent. Practice with various needle designs featured below to find the ones you like best.

The higher the size number, the smaller the needle diameter. Choose the smallest needle you can comfortably use to make the smallest, most inconspicuous stitches for hand appliqué. Use a needle threader for the smaller needles.

Betweens

Betweens needle are the shortest and are what many quilters use for hand quilting.

Sharps

Sharps needles are slightly longer and easier to use for many appliquérs.

Straw or Milliner's

Straw or Milliner's needles are even longer and are frequently used for needle-turned appliqué.

Chenille

Chenille needles are very large with a sharp point and are used to carry decorative threads to the back of the appliqué.

Irons

Use a full-size iron to prepare your background and to work with larger machine appliqué pieces. It is important to press out any creases before you add fused appliqué to a background. A medium- or travel-size iron is helpful when turning under edges of appliqué. A mini iron is useful for tacking fused appliqué to a background. Be very careful with the mini iron as both the shaft and the point heat.

Keep your iron clean from residue from fabric and fusible web. Some irons come with a nonstick coating which helps clean up mistakes with fusible web. To help keep your iron and ironing board free of fusible web accidents, use a nonstick pressing sheet, page 18, both under and on top of the appliqué. Or, pin a piece of muslin to the ironing surface and discard it as it gets sticky.

Mini Iron

Scissors

Scissors are available in many styles, sizes, and qualities. Purchase the best quality you can. Some scissors have a knife edge or a very fine serrated edge. Sharp points or blunt tips make some jobs easier. For doing a lot of continuous cutting, the handle grip is important. Some scissors have a spring release which makes cutting for long periods easier.

Use smaller scissors for cutting small pieces. For clipping curves, use small scissors with a very sharp point that will cut one thread at a time.

Duckbill scissors, sometimes called appliqué scissors, are for closely trimming away the back with protection to the appliqué.

Although normal-weight papers will not dull your scissors, use separate scissors for cutting plastic template material and cardboard.

Thread

Threads available to appliquérs and quilters come in many different colors, textures, and fiber contents. The end use will dictate the threads you will choose.

Thread spools are usually marked with the size and ply of the thread. The higher the size number, the smaller the thread diameter. The ply number indicates the number of fine yarns that are twisted together. Some thread spools state what the threads are designed for: embroidery, quilting, bobbin, etc. Spools are also marked with the fiber content.

Cotton

There are a wide variety of cotton threads available. Cotton comes in a wide range of colors, and it is easy to match almost any appliqué fabric. Spools for the sewing machine range from fine embroidery 80/2 (which is difficult to find) to 12/2. For most machine appliqué techniques, use 60/2 or 50/2 embroidery thread. For heavier stitching use 30/2 or 12/2. For hand appliqué use 60/2 embroidery thread.

Monofilament

Monofilament nylon or polyester threads are size .004 mm and are usually labeled "invisible." Use this thread for invisible machine appliqué stitching, page 56. This is the same thread you might have on hand for invisible machine quilting. The sheen of the thread varies by brand so experiment for the look you prefer.

Silk

Silk thread is very fine and makes a nearly invisible hand-appliqué stitch. Silk is more costly than cotton but, because it is so fine does not need to closely match the fabric color. Purchase a few basic colors and neutrals.

Rayon and Polyester

Rayon and polyester threads come in a variety of sizes usually ranging from 40- to 30-weight. These threads often have more luster than cotton and therefore are more decorative. Rayon threads seem to blend well with more shades of appliqué fabric and do not have as defined an edge as cotton after stitching. This can be a plus when blending colors in decorative stitching. Man-made fibers come in more decorative threads, such as metallics and ribbon-like polyester film. Practice with these threads for decorative stitching.

Refer to stitch types in *Stitching* and *Embellishing* for more thread-use suggestions.

Bobbin Thread

There are a variety of thread choices to use in the bobbin. For ease when working with 60/2 or 50/2 embroidery cotton threads, match the bobbin thread to the top thread. You will probably not have to adjust the sewing machine tension to get a perfect looking stitch. If you will be changing top thread color frequently, it is more convenient to choose one thread for the bobbin. The sewing machine tension may need to be adjusted so that none of the bobbin thread shows on top.

For decorative stitching, such as satin zigzag and free-motion embroidery, where there is a heavy build up of thread, a fine bobbin-weight thread works best. Use polyester 80/2 to 120/2 bobbin thread. Because these threads are so thin, you may have to lower the top tension almost to 0, thread the bobbin thread through the pigtail on your bobbin case, and/or tighten the bobbin case tension.

Variety of Threads for Appliqué

equipment & supplies

Fabric

Most fabric used for appliqué is 100% cotton. There is a wide variety of choices in color, print, and thread count in our quilt shops and fabric stores. Any fabric used for piecing can be used for appliqué. Thread count is the number of yarns per inch in both the crosswise and lengthwise directions. For many projects the thread count may not be as important as color. For fusible appliqué or appliqué with turned edges, any cotton fabric may be used, although fabric with low thread count may shift and be more difficult to work with. Fabric with a high thread count, such as batik, keeps a crisp edge for fusible and turned-edge appliqué for either machine or hand stitching.

If your project is going to be washed, you will want to test fabrics for colorfastness. If one fabric is prewashed, then all fabrics should be prewashed. Iron the fabrics before using for any type of appliqué. Do not spray with starch or sizing as this may prevent freezer paper from adhering when doing some types of preparation for appliqué.

For a uniform-looking finished project the background fabric should have a similar or greater thread count. On a very low thread-count background with very high thread-count appliqué pieces, the background may pucker when stitched.

There are many other types of fabric that can be used for appliqué. Silks, polyesters, and rayons will have different stitching and care requirements. For wall hangings or quilts that will not be washed, any fabric can be used. Make a sample with each fabric to find which method of appliqué works best. Test the method, thread, needles, and stitches.

When selecting fabrics for an appliqué project, look for contrast in value among the colors. For most appliqué pieces, select hand-dyed or slightly mottled-looking prints, tone-on-tone prints, or solids. These will add texture to your quilt without the fabric pattern interfering with the shape of the appliqué pieces.

Fabric Samples

Permanent and Temporary Adhesives

Paper-backed fusible web

Paper-backed fusible web has revolutionized appliqué for many quilters. Trace directly on the paper backing, fuse to the wrong side of fabric, cut out, remove paper, fuse to the background, and you are ready to stitch. There are no pins getting in the way and usually the stitching is done by machine. Follow manufacturer's instructions for iron temperature and pressing times.

Test several brands to find the one you like. Brands differ with the temperature-and-time requirements for

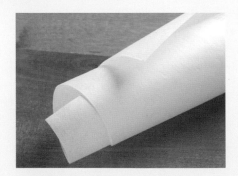

Paper-backed Fusible Web

pressing. Even within a brand there are papers designed with varying amounts of adhesive for different purposes. For appliqué to have a soft appearance, use the lightest-weight paper-backed fusible web and window the paper and

adhesive, page 24. For very flat wall hangings, leave the fusible web on the back of the entire appliqué piece and do not remove any stabilizer that may be added for special stitching.

Mark the paper of the paper-backed fusible webside with an ultra-fine point permanent marker or pencil. A permanent marker will not rub off; a pencil may smudge and even rub off onto light-colored fabrics.

Spray Adhesive

Temporary spray adhesive can be used for large pieces of fabric. Follow manufacturer's instructions and spray in a ventilated area with the work surface protected from the adhesive.

Spray the back of the appliqué piece. Then position on the background. You will be able to reposition the piece a few times. If you are working with small appliqué pieces, the propellant may scatter the appliqué.

Other Adhesives

Other adhesives used for machine and hand appliqué techniques include fabric glue sticks, liquid fabric glue, and spray starch. Read the labels to purchase a glue that is washable and acid free.

If any adhesive products gum up your needle, use rubbing alcohol to clean it.

Stabilizers

Stabilizing is essential for many machine-appliqué techniques. The thin layer of adhesive in fusible web acts as a stabilizer for fine zigzag stitching. For wider stitches and stitching through only one or two layers of fabric without any fusible adhesive, use a temporary or permanent stabilizer and/or a wooden hoop.

Temporary Stabilizers

Temporary stabilizers can be carefully torn, cut, ironed, or washed away. For sheet stabilizers place a piece the full size of your background or just slightly larger than the size of the appliqué pieces behind the appliqué. Use pins or temporary spray adhesive to hold in place. Carefully remove stabilizer after stitching.

Liquid Stabilizers

Apply liquid stabilizer (including starch) according to manufacturer's directions. Before using water-soluble or liquid stabilizers, consider if you will be washing the finished piece.

Embroidery Hoops

Wooden or plastic embroidery hoops are especially useful for decorative stitching on appliqué to keep the background taut while stitching.

For machine stitching, use a hoop along with temporary or permanent stabilizer for maximum hold. Look for a strong screw mechanism because the appliqué may have several layers of fabric and/or stitching. 7" or 8" round is the easiest size to use. Anything larger will not give you room to move the hoop around between the needle and the head of the machine, and a smaller hoop limits the stitching space.

Test several varieties of stabilizers and choose the one appropriate for your project.

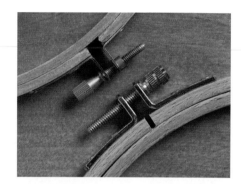

Screw Mechanism (lower hoop features stronger screw mechanism)

Temporary Sheet Stabilizers

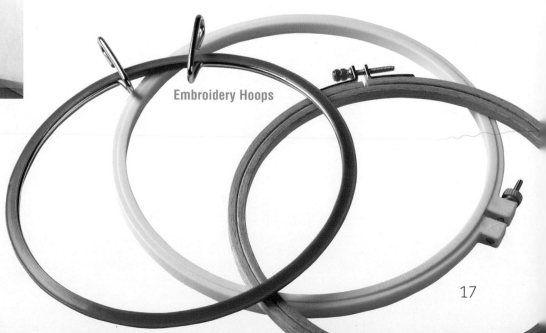

Embroidery Hoops

equipment & supplies

Template Materials

Freezer paper is used for several methods of appliqué preparation. Tag board, light-weight cardboard, and file folders can be used to make templates for the marked-line technique. Standard plastic template material is the same as used for making piecing and quilting templates. Heat-resistant template plastic is used when ironing is used in appliqué preparation.

Investigate the different methods of preparing appliqué pieces in *Prepare Appliqué* and choose the appropriate template material.

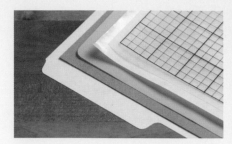

Template Materials

Overlay Papers

For appliqué designs with many layers, you may want to prepare an overlay to aid in placement of the appliqué pieces. Trace the design onto light-weight clear vinyl, sheet protectors, transparency film, tracing or tissue paper, or light-weight nonwoven tracing material with a permanent marker. For large designs use vinyl, tissue paper, or nonwoven tracing material. See pages 43 and 45.

Overlay Papers

Pins

Purchase the best pins possible. Sharp points and a metal that will not rust are important. Glass-heads on pins will not melt if ironed. For securing pieces for hand appliqué, short pins will not interfere with stitching.

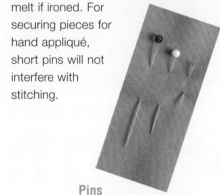

Pins

Non-stick Pressing Sheets

When working with paper backed fusible web, care needs to be taken to prevent your iron and ironing board from getting sticky with adhesive. You can protect the work surface with nonstick coated woven or plastic sheets, or use cooking parchment paper. All are slightly transparent so you can see a layout through the sheet allowing you to fuse all or part of an appliqué motif (page 44). After fusing a motif, allow it to cool before removing from the sheet.

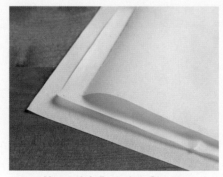

Non-stick Pressing Sheets

Marking Tools

Marking tools come in many varieties and are selected for a specific use. A mechanical pencil will keep a sharp point. It can be used on paper, template materials, and many fabrics. An ultra-fine point permanent marker can be used on all template materials and when dry will not smudge. There are many specialty markers for fabric including liquids and chalk. Choose them for color and ease of use.

Marking Tools

Light Box

The light coming through a hard surface makes tracing or positioning pattern pieces for appliqué easier. Purchase a light box at an art supply or craft store.

You can make your own light box by putting a light under a glass top table, in a shallow drawer topped with a glass or acrylic top, or under your acrylic sewing table. In daylight a window works well, especially if your project is small.

Light Box

Other Tools

Many other tools are helpful in preparing and stitching appliqué.

Thimble

For hand appliqué, practice with a thimble or thimble pads (small leather pads to put on the area of the finger used to push the needle).

Hand Stitching Tools

Wooden Pick

For needle-turn appliqué, a round wooden toothpick, shown here made from bamboo, is helpful for turning under the edge rather than using a needle, page 61.

Hemostat

A hemostat is a surgical tool turned multipurpose. Open the hemostat like scissors. Close the tip over something you want to hold together or pull and press the handles together. The handle end will latch. Once attached you can concentrate on moving the whole tool rather than having to also think about griping with the handles.

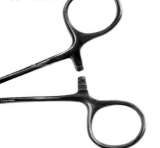

Hemostat

Stiletto

A stiletto is very useful when machine stitching to control the points of appliqué, hold yarns and other threads in place, and to guide fabric when piecing. Stilettos come in metal and bamboo.

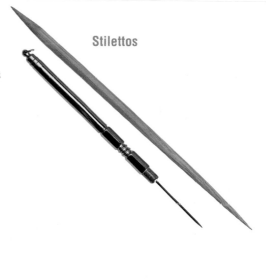

Stilettos

Workspace

Good light is essential for both machine and hand appliqué. At the machine, add extra light both in front and back to eliminate shadows. There are several styles of lamps with full-spectrum, true-color light bulbs. These are portable and can be moved to your favorite spot for hand work.

A design wall is useful for arranging appliqué pieces and laying out blocks. Cover a wall or a large piece of plywood, solid insulation, or foamcore with felt, flannel, or low-loft batting. The texture of these materials will hold some fabrics without pins.

Rotary Cutting Tools

A good acrylic ruler, rotary cutter and matt are important to cutting backgrounds, sashing and binding for your appliqué projects. These tools are also used to cut bias strips for stems.

preparing
appliqué

Decide whether you'll begin with machine or hand appliqué. Then choose from numerous options for preparing your appliqué pieces such as turned-edge, paper-backed fusible web, and needle turn. Depending on the complexity of your layout, select an arranging method that works best for your appliqué pieces.

preparing the appliqué pieces

After choosing a project, decide what type of appliqué stitching technique you would like to use—machine or hand. Then, use this chapter to investigate a preparation technique for your stitching.

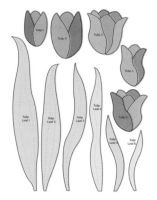

Tulip Pattern

The patterns are found in *Patterns*, pages 112–141. Trace them as directed for your choice of preparation techniques.

This chapter has several methods of preparation for machine appliqué, including using paper-backed fusible web and turning under the edges. For hand appliqué choose one of the techniques of preparation that is exclusively for hand appliqué or one of the several turned-edge methods.

Review all of the techniques and try a few. Each preparation method gives advice on what stitching techniques might be used and some of the advantages and drawbacks. Also, decide the shape of your appliqué pieces. Shape options are included in *Patterns,* pages 112–141. Intricate shapes are appropriate for paper-backed fusible web and machine stitching. A pattern with smoother lines would be better for hand appliqué and other turned-edge techniques.

The Notebooks and Tips shown here illustrate some of the basics that are used in many preparation techniques.

notebook

Tracing patterns

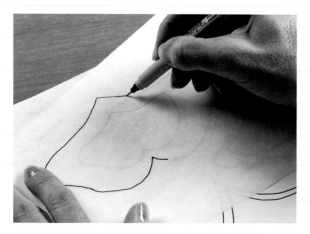

When marking patterns on template plastic, paper-backed fusible web, or freezer paper, use an ultra-fine point permanent marker. A pencil can be used on the papers but may smudge.

Marking patterns

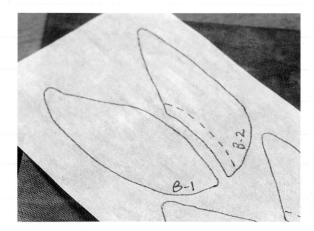

After tracing a pattern, transfer information from the pattern to the template. Make note of the pattern name or letter, number, and overlap lines or Xs. This information is for reference while building appliqué motifs and layouts.

For smooth turned-edge appliqué

Cut the edges of plastic and freezer paper templates as smoothly as possible. This is the edge your fabric edges will be turned over.

If edges are not smooth after turning, loosen fabric from the template in that area, remoisten, and redistribute the fabric.

- - - - - - - - - - - - - - - - - - - -

To prevent creases

Press all fabrics smooth before beginning to make appliqué pieces. Any creases from folding will be difficult to remove later.

Tracing around template

To prevent fabric slipping when tracing around a template, place the fabric on 220-grit sandpaper. Trace around template with a pencil or fabric marker.

Layering shapes for turned-edge techniques

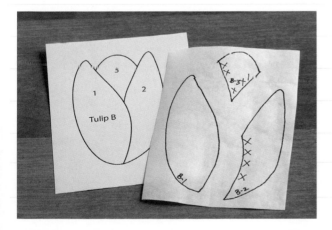

For flowers and some other appliqué motifs, the appliqué pieces will be layered. When tracing shapes where one appliqué piece will be placed under another, that underlap edge is marked with Xs.

Use your preferred method to turn under the edges, leaving the X-marked edges unturned. This minimizes the bulk of fabric on the overlapped edges.

23

paper-backed fusible web appliqué

Paper-backed fusible web preparation is used for machine appliqué. This is the quickest method of preparation, and is especially good for pieces with intricate edges that would be difficult to turn under. Fine and satin zigzag, blanket, and straight stitches are stitched on fused appliqué edges.

Trace appliqué pieces that will be cut from the same fabric about ⅛" apart.

Place lightweight paper-backed fusible web paper-side up on the appliqué pattern. Trace each pattern piece, making ⅛" extensions as necessary for underlap. Mark the pattern name or number near an edge of the pattern.

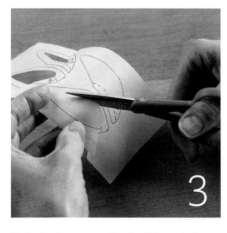

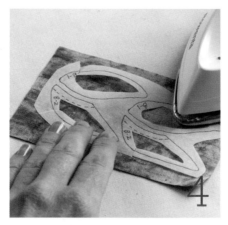

If desired, remove the fusible web from the center of the larger pattern pieces. Cut through the edge into the center of the pattern. Cut out the center leaving a scant ¼" inside the traced line. This makes the center softer to touch and in appearance. This technique of cutting out the center of the paper-backed fusible web is called "windowing."

Cut away excess fusible web about ⅛" from the traced lines. Fuse patterns to wrong side of fabric, following manufacturer's directions. Each brand of fusible web comes with instructions detailing pressing times and iron temperatures.

Cut out appliqué pieces on the traced line. Do not remove paper backing until just before arranging appliqué pieces. This preserves the pattern reference. If you are working with hand-dyed or batik fabrics where it is difficult to tell the right side, this will also help tell which side should be down and prevent a gummed-up iron surface.

Fussy cutting fabric motifs

 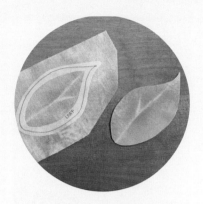 

If you want to have a specific printed motif or color shading on an appliqué piece, trace and cut out the center of the pattern. Move it around on the fabric to find the special area.

Paper-backed fusible web
For paper-backed fusible web, use the fusible web pattern for the testing and fuse in place on the wrong side of the fabric.

Turned-edge techniques
For turned-edge techniques, mark the desired area. Trace, cut out, and proceed as directed for your technique.

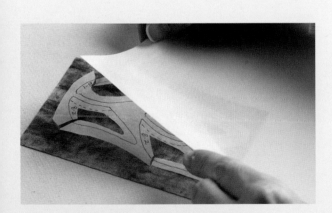

Protect your iron and ironing board
To prevent fusible web from gumming up the surface of your iron, cover the appliqué patterns with a non-stick pressing sheet both as you are pressing web to wrong side of appliqué fabric and as you are arranging the layout.

Removing paper backing
If you do not window the fusible web, it may be difficult to find an edge of paper to pull away. Drag a pin across the fused pattern piece, cutting the paper but not the fabric. This creates an edge of paper to hold and tear away.

turned edge—template and starch

This turned-edge method is very versatile and can be used with any invisible, blanket, or zigzag machine stitching and for hand appliqué. It is especially useful if you are making several of the same motif and reuse the plastic template several times.

Place heat resistant plastic template material over pattern. Trace individual pattern piece. Mark Xs on underlap edges. (Notebook, page 23.) Mark with pattern name or number. Cut out on traced line.

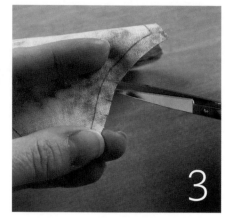

Place prepared template on wrong side of appliqué fabric. Trace around the template. Trim fabric a scant ¼" outside marked line.

Clip inside curves around the edge of the appliqué shape. When clipping inside curves, clip about halfway to the edge of the line. Do not clip any underlap edges (marked with Xs). To prevent fraying, make clips on the bias of the fabric. (Notebook, page 31.)

Clip inside points straight into the point to within one thread of the line.

Spray some spray starch into a dish or saucer. Use a small brush to moisten the seam-allowance edge with starch except for the underlap X-marked sections. To protect table surface, place appliqué piece on parchment or freezer paper.

Working in small sections, press fabric edges over template edge with the tip of a hot iron. On outside curves make very small tucks (pleats) in the fabric. Do not press up the seam allowance on edges marked with Xs.

For a sharp outside point, begin by pressing the excess fabric at the tip directly over the point.

Then, press the seam allowance in from one side.

tip

Cutting template plastic
Do not use your best fabric scissors for cutting template plastic. Use medium-duty scissors that will not be ruined by the tough plastic.

Now, press the seam allowance in from the other side, completing the sharp point.

After pressing the seam allowance over the template, turn over and press on the right side. Cool. Loosen template and remove. Repress.

turned edge—freezer paper and glue

For a very crisp edge try this preparation technique. Using your fingertips rather than an iron makes it easier to turn curves and points. Stitch with blind hem invisible machine stitching, page 56. The paper must be removed after stitching.

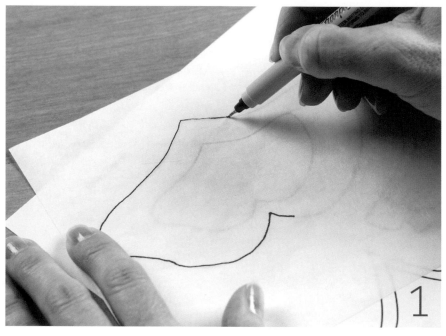

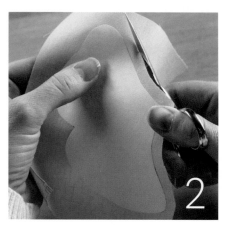

Press freezer paper pattern shiny-side down to wrong side of appliqué fabric. Trim fabric a scant ¼" outside freezer paper pattern.

Place freezer paper matte-side up on pattern. Trace individual pattern piece. Mark Xs on underlap edges. (Notebook, page 23.) Mark with pattern name or number. Cut out on traced line.

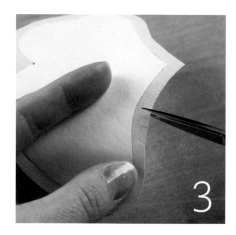

Clip inside curves around the edge of the appliqué shape. When clipping inside curves, clip about halfway to the edge of the pattern. Do not clip any underlap edges (marked with Xs). To prevent fraying, make clips on the bias of the fabric. (Notebook, page 31.)

Clip inside points straight into the point to within 1 thread of the pattern.

Using a washable glue stick, apply glue to the seam allowance edge except for the underlap sections. To protect table surface, place appliqué piece on parchment or freezer paper.

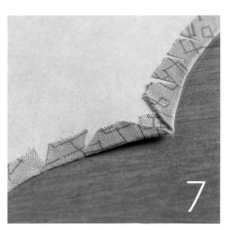

Working in small sections, finger-press fabric edges over paper edge. Use the tip of your thumb on top and index finger underneath. On outside curves make very small tucks (pleats) in the fabric. Do not finger-press the seam allowance on edges marked with Xs.

For a sharp outside point, begin by pressing the excess fabric at the tip directly over the point. Press the seam allowance in from one side. Then, press the other seam allowance in, making a sharp point. (See Steps 7–9, page 27.)

Allow glue to dry completely before arranging appliqué pieces.

Removing the freezer paper after stitching

After stitching completely around appliqué, (page 56), the paper must be removed. From the wrong side, carefully trim away the background fabric to about ¼" from stitching line. Moisten stitched edges to loosen glue. Carefully remove freezer paper.

notebook

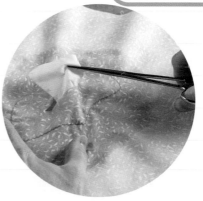

For simple shapes

You may be able to remove paper from simple shapes through a slit in the background fabric rather than trimming it away. A hemostat helps get a firm grip on the paper.

turned edge—freezer paper pinned to wrong side

This method makes it easy to position appliqué pieces before stitching. The shiny side of the freezer paper will stick temporarily to the background and pins may not be needed if stitching only one motif. Stitch with blind hem invisible machine stitching (page 56) or hand appliqué (page 58).

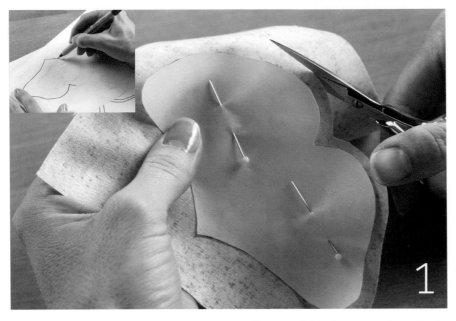

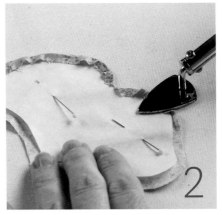

Place freezer paper shiny side up on pattern. Trace individual pattern piece. Mark Xs on underlap edges. (Notebook, page 23.) Mark with pattern name or number. Cut out on traced line. Pin freezer paper pattern shiny side up to wrong side of fabric. Trim fabric a scant ¼" outside freezer-paper pattern.

Proceed with steps #3–6 from Turned Edge—Freezer Paper and Glue on page 28. Press fabric edges over paper edge with the tip of a hot iron. It is not necessary to use glue. The coating on the shiny side of the freezer paper acts as a temporary adhesive.

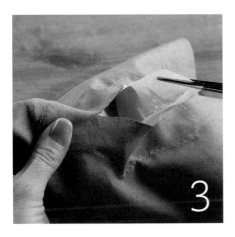

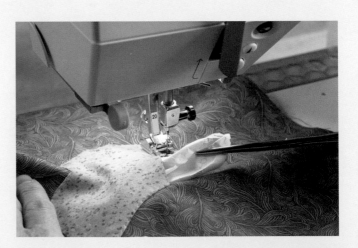

Remove freezer paper after stitching as described in Notebook: For Simple Shapes on page 29. It is not necessary to moisten the stitched edges. Grip the paper with hemostat or tweezers and jiggle to loosen. Pull out.

Step 3 option Stitch around the appliqué piece leaving about 2" unstitched. Lift presser foot and with a hemostat or stiletto loosen freezer paper from under appliqué piece. Carefully remove through opening. Complete stitching.

Several special cutting techniques will make your turned-edge appliqué smooth and crisp and the points sharp.

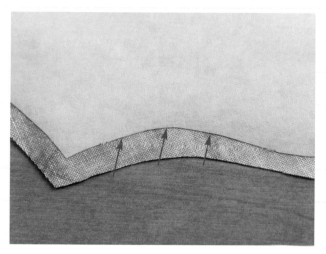

Clipping inside curves

Look closely at the fabric grain on the seam allowance. Make clips through the bias at a 45° angle to the direction of the fabric threads (not always at a 90° angle to the pattern edge).

Clipping outside curves

If an outside curve is very narrow or almost pointed, you may need to take small V-shaped cuts in the seam allowance. This will allow the excess fabric to lay flat instead of overlapping.

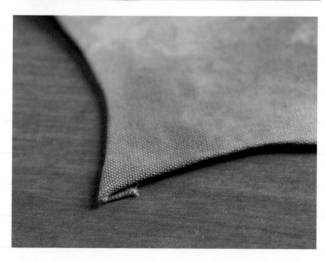

Trimming points

If the point is very acute, you may need to trim some of the seam allowance fabric from one side on the back. This photo shows fabric that needs trimming.

turned edge—freezer paper ironed to right side

Use freezer paper as a guide for turning edges under. The paper is removed before stitching making this method very versatile. Use with invisible, blanket, or zigzag machine stitching or hand appliqué.

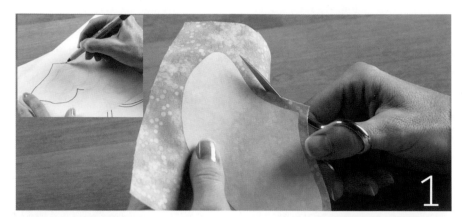

Place freezer paper shiny-side up on pattern. Trace individual pattern piece. Mark Xs on underlap edges. (Notebook, page 23.) Mark with pattern name or number. Cut out on traced line. Press freezer paper pattern shiny-side down to right side of fabric. Trim a scant ¼" outside freezer paper pattern.

Proceed with steps #3–6 from Turned Edge—Freezer Paper and Glue technique on page 28. Use the freezer paper edge as a guide to finger press the glued seam allowance to the wrong side away from the freezer paper. Let glue dry. Remove freezer paper before stitching.

tip

Lining Light Colors

When light-colored appliqué overlaps darker colors, there is often a shadow. To prevent this, line the lighter appliqué pieces with the same color or white fabric.

For turned edge preparation techniques, cut a piece of the same color or white fabric the exact size of the appliqué pattern. Insert this lining behind appliqué piece before stitching.

For paper-backed fusible web preparation technique, make duplicate tracings. Fuse the appliqué fabric to the lining fabric, lining up the pattern. Cut out using the line on the lining fabric.

faced technique

The faced method of preparing appliqué pieces is especially effective for larger appliqué pieces with simple shapes. The prepared appliqué pieces can be arranged on the background and stitched with any machine stitching. The water soluble stabilizer will later dissolve during washing.

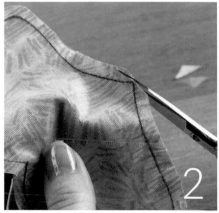

Place water soluble stabilizer on pattern. Trace individual pattern pieces. Mark Xs on underlap edges. (Notebook, page 23.) Mark with pattern name or number. Place marked facing, on right side of a similar size piece of appliqué fabric. Stitching on the marked line, sew the pieces together using a smaller than normal stitch length. Use a thread color to blend with the appliqué fabric.

Trim seam allowance to ¼". This trimming may be done with pinking shears. Clip inside and outside curves around the edge of the appliqué shape about half way to the stitched line. Clip inside points straight into the point to within one thread of the line. Trim points straight across about ¹⁄₁₆" from the point and then at a slight angle.

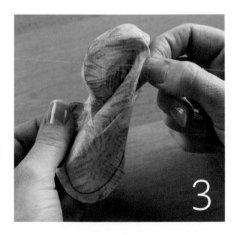

Make a slit in the center of the facing material, being careful not to cut through the appliqué fabric. Carefully turn appliqué inside out through the slit, using a hemostat, if desired. If this piece has an unstitched edge, use that to turn inside out.

Finger press to make flat, then press with an iron from the right side. Water soluble facing material may get stiff or distort if it gets too hot or is ironed directly. Trim away the center of the water soluble facing material, leaving the pressed fabric edge.

Option: For facing use lightweight nonfusible nonwoven interfacing. After trimming, grade seam allowance so the interfacing is slightly smaller than the appliqué fabric; clip curves and points. Slit facing and turn inside out.

marked line for hand appliqué

With a minimum of preparation you are ready to position your appliqué pieces. There is no paper to remove after stitching. Try this technique and freezer-paper template technique below for hand appliqué needle turn preparation to see which you like best.

tip

Marking tools

Pick a pencil or other marker that allows you to clearly see the marked line on your fabric. (Marking tools page 18.)

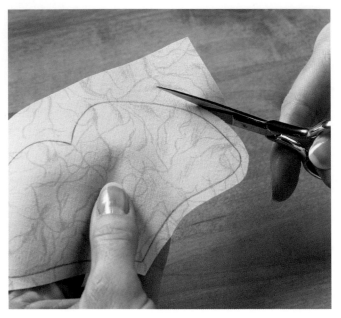

Place template material or freezer paper shiny-side up on pattern. Trace individual pattern pieces. Mark Xs on underlap edges. (Notebook, page 23.) Cut out template on traced line. Flip template material over or place freezer pattern shiny side down on right side of fabric. Trace around pattern with pencil or other marker. Remove pattern. Trim fabric a scant ¼" outside marked line.

freezer-paper template for hand appliqué

A freezer-paper template fused to the right side of your appliqué fabric is the fastest way to get pieces ready for hand stitching. Because there is no drawn line, variations in shape are not noticeable.

Place freezer paper shiny side up on pattern. Trace individual pattern piece. Mark Xs on underlap edges. (Notebook, page 23.) Mark with pattern name or number. Cut out on traced line. Press pattern shiny side down on right side of fabric. Trim fabric a scant ¼" outside freezer paper pattern. After stitching, you may be able to use the pattern a few more times.

turned edge—thread basted

Thread-basting is frequently the preparation choice for hand appliqué of more complicated shapes. Preparation time is longer, but the appliqué pieces are easy to position and stitch. This method can also be used with any machine stitching.

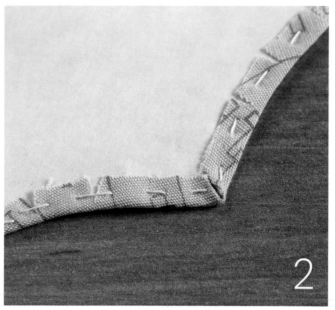

Prepare the appliqué piece as for Turned Edge—Freezer Paper and Glue on page 28 steps #1–4. Thread needle with light-colored thread. Start with the knot on the front of the piece. Working in small sections, turn the fabric edges over the paper edge and baste through all layers. On outside curves make small tucks in the fabric; clip inside curves. Do not turn the seam allowances on edges marked with Xs.

For a sharp point, finger-press the excess fabric at the tip directly over the point. Finger-press the seam allowance in from one side and baste. Finger-press the other seam allowance, making a sharp point. Continue basting. (See Steps 7–9, page 27.) After stitching appliqué piece to background, take out basting and remove paper following Step 3, on page 30.

notebook

Turning a perfect circle

Trace around a heat resistant plastic circle template on the wrong side of the fabric. Cut out a scant ¼" beyond circle. Knot a short length of thread. Make running stitches between the traced circle and the edge.

Pull on the thread end to gather the edges around the circle template. Smooth out the gathers. Take a backstitch to hold in place. Apply spray starch, if desired. Firmly press the edges.

Loosen the gathering and remove the template. Re-press, if necessary. Template may be used many times.

Reverse appliqué with paper-backed fusible web

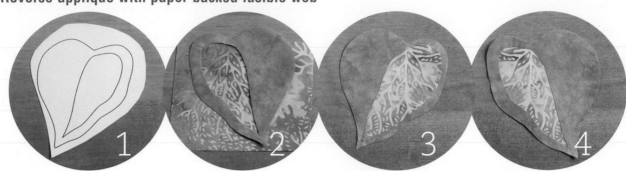

Select a pattern where the reverse appliqué will give a unique effect, i.e., one side of a leaf, animal eyes, or an appliqué part you want to appear to recede. Trace, fuse, and cut out the top appliqué piece including cutting away the open section.

Select a fabric for the under fabric. This could be a fussy-cut piece. Cut the under fabric about ¼" larger than the open section.

Fuse under fabric to wrong side of appliqué piece, being sure to leave at least a ⅛" rim of fabric on the outside edge of the top appliqué piece.

For small pieces fuse the unit to the background, then stitch around the reverse appliqué. For large pieces, stitch around the reverse appliqué edge before positioning on background.

Reverse appliqué with turned edges

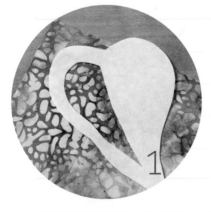
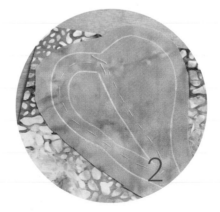
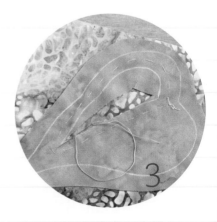

Select a pattern where the reverse appliqué will give a unique effect, i.e., one side of a leaf, animal eyes, or an appliqué part you want to appear to recede. Select a fabric for the under fabric. This could be a fussy-cut piece.

Trace the template on the right side of the top fabric. Baste around the reverse appliqué shape about ¼" away from the edge to be turned under.

Slit the center of the top fabric in the area to be reversed. Turn under at the marked line and stitch, clipping and turning as directed for curves, points, and corners, page 60. Remove basting, trim excess under-fabric, and stitch as a unit to background.

36

bias stems

Stems are frequently the first appliqué pieces to be positioned on a background. Fabric for curved stems needs to be cut on the bias. This allows the stem to curve without tucks or puckers. There are several methods for making bias stems. They all start with finding the bias of your fabric.

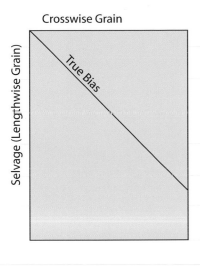

Finding the true bias

Trim fabric on the crosswise grain line. Fold the cut edge over to meet the selvage (lengthwise grain). This diagonal fold is the true bias. Lay a ruler slightly inside this fold and cut off the fold. The resulting edges can be used for cutting bias strips.

Or, use the 45° angle line on your ruler. Place ruler with the 45° line along the selvage. Make a cut and then use these edges to cut bias strips.

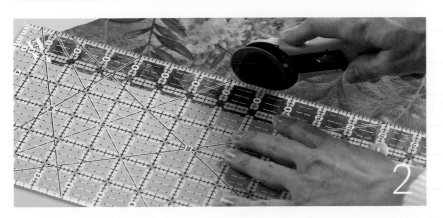

Cutting bias strips

Position ruler the desired strip width from the cut edge. Cut bias strips.

bias stems—paper-backed fusible web

This method can be used with any appliqué method. Most frequently it is used when the appliqué method uses paper-backed fusible web. It is easy to cut very narrow stems.

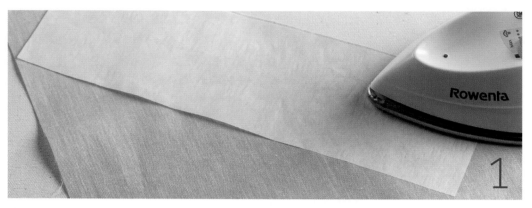

Find the true bias of the stem fabric. Cut a piece of paper-backed fusible web a little longer and wider than the total measurements of the stems needed. Following manufacturer's directions, press paper-backed fusible web to the wrong side of the stem fabric near the bias edge.

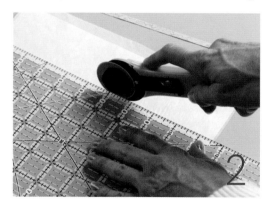

Trim off the edge of the fabric and fusible web. Cut stems desired width.

Mark the stem position on the background. Following manufacturer's directions, press bias stem into position over the line.

> **tip**
>
> ### Cutting stems
> Stems can be cut at a slight angle to make them taper from wide to narrow.

bias stems—single fold

The single-fold method is the simplest of the folded bias stems. One side of the stem is machine or handstitched to the background.

Find the true bias of the stem fabric (Notebook, page 37) Cut strips 2 times desired final width plus ½". (For a ⅜"-wide stem cut 1¼"-wide strip.) Fold strips in half wrong sides together and press.

Cut to required stem lengths plus a few inches for ease. Mark the stem position on appliqué background. Place the cut edges on the marked line. Pin or baste in place. Machine or handstitch ¼" from cut edges.

Fold stem over stitching and seam allowance. Press lightly. Pin or baste in place.

tips

Trimming narrow stems

If the finished stem is smaller than ¼", position the stem strip on top of the marked stem position line. After stitching, trim away the excess seam allowance before folding stem over stitches.

Curving stems

If the stem only has one curve, place the cut edges on the marked line with the fold positioned to the inside of the curve. (Do not stretch.) When folded over, the folded bias edge will stretch to the outside curve. If stem has curves in both directions, ease the fabric as you position it on the outside of the curve.

bias stems—folded tube

This tube method gives a smooth single fold to both edges of the stem. Use metal or heat-resistant plastic bias bars to aid in preparation.

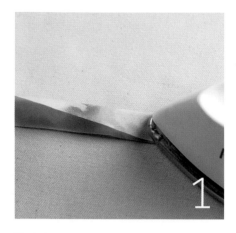

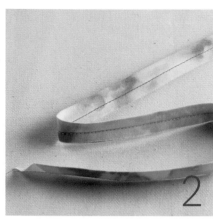

Find the true bias of the stem fabric (Notebook, page 37.) Cut strips 2 times desired final width plus ½". (For a ⅜" wide stem cut 1¼"- wide strip.) Fold strips in half wrong sides together and press.

Stitch lengthwise ¼" from cut edges.

Roll the resulting tube so the seam is near the center. Trim seam allowance, if necessary so it does not stick out beyond either rolled edge. Press.

Mark the stem position on appliqué background. Pin or baste stem in place straddling the marked line.

If desired, insert the proper size bias bar and press. Cut to required stem lengths plus a few inches for ease.

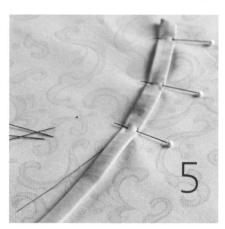

Bias bars

bias stems—triple fold

Triple fold bias makes very even, smooth stems with no seams on the underneath side. Stems can be prepared quickly and positioned on the background easily.

Find the true bias of the stem fabric (Notebook, page 37.) Cut strips 3 times desired final width. (For a ⅜" wide stem cut 1⅛"-wide strip.) With wrong sides together, finger press ⅓ of the width up. Fold remaining fabric over first edge, folding the strip in thirds. Press.

Cut to required stem lengths plus a few inches for ease. Mark the stem position on appliqué background. Pin or baste stem in place straddling the line.

> notebook

Folding long strips for bias stems

Make triple-fold bias stems in long lengths for border vines and other long stems.

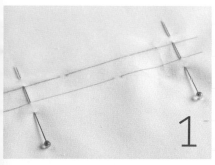

Draw a 4" line near the middle of an 8" square of muslin. Draw another line the stem width away and parallel to the first. Position 2 long straight pins about 3" apart, inserting as shown above, forming a tunnel the width of the stem. Pin the muslin to your ironing board.

Sew bias strips together to make longer strips, if desired. At one end of the strip start the folding as above by folding in ⅓ of the width from one side and folding over another ⅓ from the other side. Finger press.

Insert the folded stem end under one pin and then the other. Place the point of your iron between the pins. Pull the bias strip through the pins feeding the unfolded end into the pin slots, letting the iron press the stem as you pull.

arranging appliqué

There are several methods for arranging prepared appliqué pieces on your background. For simple layouts, center the motifs or arrange in quadrants. For more complicated layouts, trace the design to put under a light background or use an overlay on top of the background.

notebook

For layouts and overlays

The layouts (groupings of patterns) found in *Patterns* and *Projects* are reduced to fit on the pages of this book. For full size, print the layouts the stated percentage on a copy machine.

Use the enlarged printout for making an overlay, page 43, or under a background, page 44.

Tulip Layout

arranging simple appliqué

For arranging prepared appliqué pieces or groupings that are centered or arranged symmetrically, the background can be folded to find the center and aid the alignment.

Idea 1 If working with a simple block and a centered or symmetrical design, fold the background in straight or diagonal quarters to find the center. Arrange the prepared appliqué pieces using the folds as a guide for accurate centering. Pin, baste, or fuse in place.

Idea 2 If you are arranging the appliqué in 4 quadrants, fold the background in straight or diagonal quarters. Arrange the prepared appliqué pieces using the folds as a guide for positioning. Pin, baste, or fuse in place.

Preparing a layout overlay

A layout overlay is a guide for arranging appliqué pieces on the background. Experiment with these methods to find your favorite. Methods 3 and 4 are best for hand appliqué because the overlay material is pliable.

Method 1

Cut a piece of tissue or tracing paper about the size of the appliqué background. Place on top of the full-sized layout. Using an ultra-fine point permanent marker, trace the motif, the center, and any other registration marks.

Method 2

Copy the motif on a home or commercial copier and print to transparency film. Or, trace the layout and markings onto transparency film with an ultra-fine point permanent marker.

Method 3

Cut a piece of clear lightweight (4mm) vinyl or acetate about the size of the appliqué background. Place on top of the full-sized layout. Using an ultra-fine point permanent marker, trace the motif, the center, and any other registration marks.

Method 4

Cut a piece of nonwoven tracing fabric about the size of the appliqué background. Place on top of the full-sized layout. Using an ultra-fine point permanent marker, trace the layout and markings.

arranging appliqué on light background

If the background for the appliqué pieces is light to medium-light, you can place the layout under the background and lightly trace directly on the background.

Tracing directly to background

Place the full-size layout on a lightbox or on a solid white surface. Center the background over the layout and with a pencil lightly trace the appliqué positions directly onto the fabric with pencil or fabric marker.

---

notebook

Arranging paper-backed fusible web appliqué

Place the layout or a reversed (traced or printed) pattern under a nonstick pressing sheet. Remove paper backing from appliqué pieces. Arrange the bottom layer of pieces on the pressing sheet. Tack into place with a hot iron to build the motif.

Continue adding appliqué pieces and press to form a unit. Cool and remove the unit from nonstick sheet.

If your background is light in value, place it on top of the layout. Arrange the remaining appliqué pieces including the fused motif on the background.

arranging complex appliqué

For arranging appliqué pieces on medium to dark backgrounds, prepare a layout overlay (Notebook, page 43). Attach the overlay on top of the background and begin adding appliqué pieces.

Arranging all appliqué pieces before stitching

Pin, tape, or baste a prepared overlay to the top of the background matching the center and any other registration marks. Lift overlay slightly and arrange prepared appliqué units and separate pieces, a few at a time.

Start with the pieces that rest completely on the background. Continue pinning, basting, or fusing appliqué pieces into place until all of the pieces are positioned.

Arranging one layer at a time

Pin, tape, or baste a prepared overlay to the top of the background matching the center and any other registration marks. Lift overlay slightly and arrange the pieces that rest completely on the background. Turn the overlay up; stitch appliqué pieces in place. Flip overlay back over, position the next layer of appliqué pieces and stitch. Continue until stitching is finished.

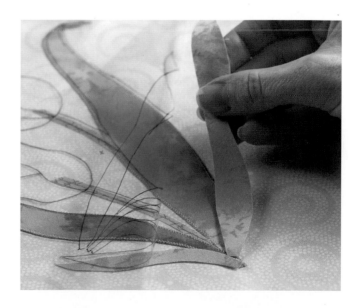

stitching

On the following pages you'll find basic stitches for attaching appliqué pieces to the background—ranging from nearly invisible to decorative— suitable for either machine or hand appliqué.

Beginning and ending stitching is the same for the machine-stitching in this chapter and most of the machine-stitching in *Embellishing.* The only time you would not use this technique is if the bobbin thread is too large to come up through the background to the top.

Beginning-machine stitching

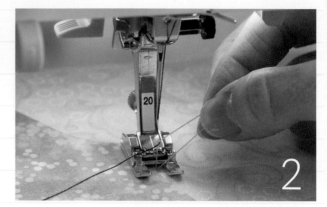

When beginning stitching, bring the bobbin thread to the top. This will prevent a snarl or knot of thread on the back of your appliqué. Take one stitch and pull on the top thread to bring the bobbin thread loop up.

Pull on the loop of bobbin thread to pull the tail to the top. Take a few locking stitches and proceed with stitching.

Ending-machine stitching

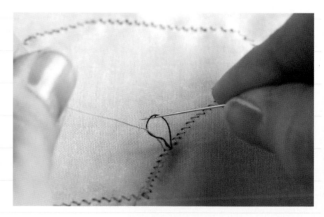

At the end of the stitching take a few very short stitches to lock the threads. Pull stitching away from the needle. Clip beginning and ending thread tails.

If you are using a contrasting thread, leave 5" tails of thread at both the beginning and ending. Pull top thread through to the back and tie a knot. If the knot does not seem to hold, fix with permanent fabric glue.

Setting up for machine-stitching and embellishing:

Most machine-stitching types have the same basic setup. Most stitching samples in this chapter are stitched with red thread to make them more visible.

- Choose a needle that works best for your combination of fabric and thread. Use a smaller needle for finer fabrics, monofilament, and finer threads, a larger for needle for decorative threads and heavier fabrics, and select a specialty needle for some decorative threads.

- Use an open toe embroidery, or appliqué presser foot to clearly see the edges, curves, and points. These feet have a wide groove on the underside to accommodate the buildup of thread.

- Use a bobbin thread that matches the top thread for easiest tension control. If changing the top color frequently or for heavy, decorative stitching such as satin zigzag, it may be helpful to use a neutral color of bobbin-weight thread, page 15. But, pay close attention to the tension.

Stabilizing for machine-stitching

It is often necessary to stabilize appliqué to prevent puckering when you sew with stitches that make wide zigzags or swings of the needle. A piece of sheet stabilizer, page 17, is placed under the appliqué and can be removed after stitching. The stitch sample in the photo shows puckering on the right line of satin zigzag stitching where there was no stabilizer. For very heavy stitching you may need both a piece of sheet stabilizer and a hoop. Carefully tear or cut away stabilizer after stitching.

fine zigzag stitch

Two types of zigzag stitches are used for machine appliqué. Fine zigzag stitches are narrow and slightly spaced while satin zigzag stitches (narrow, wide, or decorative) are spaced very closely together.

Fine zigzag stitching is recommended for fusible-web-backed appliqué because the fused adhesive is already holding the fabric to the background. Fine zigzag may also be used for turned edge techniques, but blind hem or blanket stitches are used more frequently.

Setup for fine zigzag stitching

- Threads used most often for fine zigzag stitching are a 60-weight cotton embroidery, 40-weight rayon, or polyester in a color matching the appliqué or monofilament invisible thread.

- In most instances a 1.5 mm-wide and .75 mm -long stitch will work best. Make a sample and test various width and length combinations. The best size stitch will depend on the size of the appliqué piece, the fabric, and the thread.

- It is usually not necessary to stabilize your project if the edges of the appliqué are fused. The adhesive of the fusible web acts as a stiff third layer much as a sheet of stabilizer would. Make a test sample to see if you need additional stabilizer.

Stitching Instructions

The fine zigzag stitch should secure just the edge of the appliqué. Position the presser foot so the right swing of the stitch will be next to the edge of the appliqué. The left swing of the needle will then come onto the appliqué. Begin stitching at the junction of 2 pieces or along a continuous edge. It is more difficult to start at an inner or outer point.

---

tip

Avoiding frayed edges

If the right swing of the fine or satin zigzag stitch is on the appliqué it may cause fraying, especially on a loosely woven fabric. If the stitches are too far to the right, the appliqué may tear out or the background may pucker.

Stitching Corners

Outside Corners

To stitch an outside corner, stitch to the end of the appliqué and stop with the needle down on the right edge. Raise the presser foot, pivot the fabric, lining up with the next side, lower the presser foot, and continue stitching.

Inside Corners

An inside corner is stitched by stitching past the corner one or two stitches. Stop with needle down on the left side. Raise the presser foot and pivot the fabric lining up with the next edge. Lower the presser foot and continue stitching. If the corner is less than 90°, move the fabric slightly so the first right stitch is within the previous stitches.

Stitching Curves

Outside Curves

When stitching outside curves, occasionally pivot the appliqué. Stop with the needle down on the right swing, raise the presser foot and pivot the appliqué slightly, lower the presser foot, and continue stitching. The tightness of the curve will dictate how often you need to pivot. If you do not pivot with the needle down on the right swing, there will be gaps in the stitches.

Inside Curves

When stitching inside curves, occasionally pivot the appliqué. Stop with the needle down on the left swing, raise the presser foot and pivot the appliqué slightly, lower the presser foot, and continue stitching. The tightness of the curve will dictate how often you need to pivot. If you do not pivot with the needle down on the left swing, there will be gaps in the stitches on the appliqué.

Stitching Points

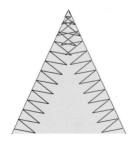

Tapered Points

For a tapered point stitch to the end of the appliqué corner, decreasing the stitch width the last few stitches and stopping with the needle down on the right edge. Raise the presser foot and pivot the fabric, lining up with the next side. Lower the presser foot, take one stitch, then gradually increase the stitch width until the stitching is at the original setting. (This will only be a few stitches.) Continue stitching.

satin zigzag stitch

The satin zigzag stitch may be used for appliqué that has a fused edge. It makes a solid line of stitching at a variety of widths. The satin zigzag stitch is more decorative than the fine zigzag stitch. It may used with a turned edge although it may get bulky.

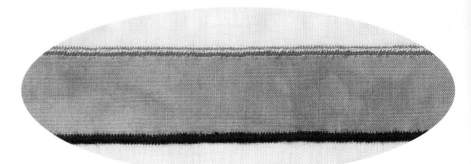

Setup for satin zigzag stitching

- Threads used most often for satin zigzag stitching are 60-weight cotton embroidery, 50-weight rayon, or polyester in matching or contrasting colors. Do not use monofilament invisible thread.

- Make a sample to test various stitch widths to achieve the look you want. The best size stitch will depend on the size of the appliqué, the fabric, the thread and the decorative purpose of the stitching. There is also some variation in stitch length within the satin zigzag stitch look. If the stitches are too close together, they may bunch up and be uneven. If the stitches are too far apart they will not have a solid satin stitch look.

Stitching Instructions

The satin zigzag stitch should secure just the edge of the appliqué. Position the presser foot so the right swing of the stitch will be next to the edge of the appliqué. The left swing of the needle will then come onto the appliqué. Begin stitching at the junction of 2 pieces or along a continuous line. It is more difficult to start at an inner or outer point.

Stitching Corners

Double-stitched Outside Corners

For a double-stitched outside corner, stitch to the end of the appliqué corner and stop with the needle down on the right edge. Raise the presser foot, pivot the fabric, lining up with the next side, lower the presser foot, and continue stitching.

Butted Outside Corners

For a butted outside corner, stitch to the end of the appliqué corner and stop with the needle down on the left swing of the stitch. Raise the presser foot, turn the handwheel until the needle moves back to the right position, and pivot the fabric, positioning the needle at the right edge of the next side. Lower the presser foot and continue stitching.

Mitered Outside Corners

For a mitered outside corner, move the needle position to the far right. Stitch to the end of the appliqué corner; stop with the needle down on the right edge. Raise the presser foot, pivot the fabric, lining up with the next side. Reduce the stitch width to almost zero. Lower the presser foot; stitching slowly, gradually increase stitch width to original setting until the stitching meets the previously stitched line. (This will only be a few stitches.) Continue stitching.

Stitching Corners

Inside Corners

An inside corner is stitched by stitching past the corner the width of the satin stitch. Stop with needle down on the left side. Raise the presser foot and pivot the fabric lining up with the next edge. Lower the presser foot and continue stitching. If the corner is less than 90°, move the fabric slightly away from you so the first right stitch is within the previous stitches.

Stitching Curves

Outside Curves

When stitching outside curves, occasionally pivot the appliqué. Stop with the needle down on the right swing, raise the presser foot and pivot the appliqué slightly, lower the presser foot, and continue stitching. The tightness of the curve will dictate how often you need to pivot. If you do not pivot with the needle down on the right swing, there will be gaps in the stitches.

Inside Curves

When stitching inside curves, occasionally pivot the appliqué. Stop with the needle down on the left swing, raise the presser foot and pivot the appliqué slightly, lower the presser foot, and continue stitching. The tightness of the curve will dictate how often you need to pivot. If you do not pivot with the needle down on the left swing, there will be gaps in the stitches on the appliqué.

Stitching Points

Tapered Points

Move the needle position to the far right. Stitch to the place near the point on the appliqué where the left swing touches the next side. Gradually decrease the stitch width, stitching to the point. Stop with the needle down on the right edge. Raise the presser foot and pivot the fabric, lining up with the next side. Lower the presser foot and stitching slowly, gradually increasing the stitch width to the original setting. Continue stitching.

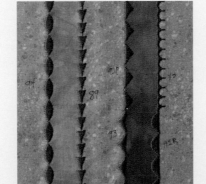

tip

Programmed satin stitches
Your machine may have other programmed satin stitches that work well on the edge of an appliqué as embellishment, page 65. Make a test sample, marking the pattern number and any changes made in the width or length.

blanket stitch

The blanket (or buttonhole) stitch can be used with fused edge or any of the turned-edge appliqué preparation methods in **Preparing Appliqué.** The blanket stitch gives a crisp look to the edges and is used to mimic *broderie perse* and other nostalgic appliqué such as Sunbonnet Sue.

Setup for Blanket stitch

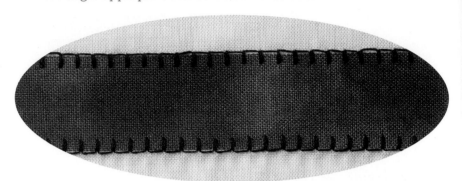

- Threads used most often for the blanket stitch are 50-weight or thicker cotton thread. Do not use monofilament invisible thread. The buttonhole stitch is used to give the edge of the appliqué a handstitched look. Traditionally the thread is black.

- The blanket stitch is a programmed stitch in most sewing machines. There may be two or more blanket stitch variations, including one that double-stitches each swing stitch or one that mirror images the stitch. Choose the best variation for your project. Make a stitch sample and test various widths and lengths to achieve the look you want. The best size stitch will depend on the size of the appliqué, the fabric, and the thread.

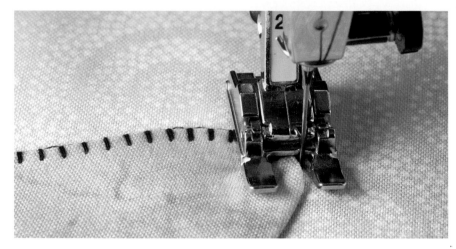

Stitching Instructions

Position the presser foot so the forward stitches of the blanket stitch are along the right edge of the appliqué but not so close that they are hidden by the appliqué edge. The left swing of the needle will then come onto the appliqué. Begin stitching at the junction of 2 pieces or along a continuous line. It is more difficult to start at an inner or outer point.

tip

Broderie perse

Broderie perse refers to a technique where individual motifs are cut from one fabric and appliquéd to another fabric foundation. Traditionally, *broderie perse* appliqué is stitched with a small blanket stitch.

Stitching Corners

Outside Corners

For an outside corner, stitch to the corner of the appliqué, stopping with the needle down at the end of a forward stitch. (You may need to adjust the fabric or stitch length as you approach the corner to get the completed forward stitch exactly at the corner.) Raise the presser foot and pivot the fabric 45°. Lower the presser foot and complete a swing to the left and back. Raise the presser foot and pivot the fabric another 45°, lining up with the next edge. Lower the presser foot and continue stitching.

Inside Corners

For an inside corner, stitch to the corner of the appliqué stopping with needle down at the end of a swing stitch. Raise the presser foot and pivot the fabric 45°. Lower the presser foot, lower the feed dogs and make the next "forward" stitch, holding the fabric so the needle goes in the same hole. Make a swing stitch. Make the forward stitch, again holding the fabric so the needle goes in the same hole. Raise the presser foot, pivot the fabric 45°, lower the presser foot, raise the feed dogs and continue stitching.

Stitching Curves

Outside Curves

When stitching outside curves, occasionally pivot the appliqué. Stop with the needle down at the end of a forward stitch, raise the presser foot and pivot the appliqué slightly, lower the presser foot, and continue stitching. The tightness of the curve will dictate how often you need to pivot. If you pivot with the needle down on the left swing, there will be gaps in the swing stitches.

Inside Curves

When stitching inside curves, occasionally pivot the appliqué. Stop with the needle down at the end of a forward stitch, raise the presser foot and pivot the appliqué slightly, lower the presser foot, and continue stitching. The tightness of the curve will dictate how often you need to pivot. If you pivot with the needle down on the left swing, there will be gaps in the swing stitches.

Stitching Points

Tapered Points

Tapered points are stitched in the same manner as the outside corners. Make the first pivot to divide the corner in half. You may need to shorten the stitch width for one stitch so the swing stitches do not cross over each other.

blind hem—invisible machine stitch

For invisible machine appliqué use the blind-hem or vari-overlock stitch. Blind-hem stitching is recommended for turned-edge appliqué to give the look and feel of hand appliqué.

Setup for blind-hem stitching

- The top thread should be monofilament invisible nylon or polyester thread.

- In the bobbin use 60-weight cotton or polyester thread in a color matching the appliqué background.

- In most instances a .1mm-wide and .1mm-long stitch will work best. There should be approximately ⅛" between bites, and each bite should catch one or two threads of the appliqué piece. Make a stitch sample and test various widths and lengths to achieve an invisible hand appliqué look. The best size stitch will depend on the size of the appliqué, the fabric, and the thread.

Stitching Instructions

The blind hem stitch has two to four straight forward stitches and 1 zigzag stitch to the left. Position the presser foot so the forward stitches are along the edge of the appliqué and the zigzag stitch will catch one to two threads of the appliqué. Begin stitching at the junction of two pieces or anywhere on a continuous line.

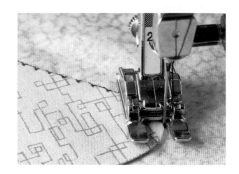

Stitching Corners

Outside Corners and Tapered Points

The outside corner is stitched by stitching to the corner of the appliqué and stopping with the needle down at the end of the forward stitches. Raise the presser foot and pivot the fabric dividing the corner in half. Lower the presser foot and complete a zigzag stitch. Raise the presser foot and pivot the fabric lining up with the next edge. Lower the presser foot and continue stitching.

Inside Corners

An inside corner is stitched by stitching to the corner of the appliqué and stopping with the needle down at the end of the forward stitches. Raise the presser foot and pivot the fabric 45°. Lower the presser foot and complete a zigzag stitch in the crotch of the corner. Raise the presser foot and pivot the fabric another 45° lining up with the next edge. Lower the presser foot and continue stitching.

Stitching Curves

No special consideration has to be given to the curves because the width and length of the stitches is so small. Gradually turn the project as you go around curves keeping the forward stitches next to the edge of the appliqué piece.

straight stitch

Straight stitching or top stitching can be used on fused-edge appliqué or appliqué with turned edges, especially faced appliqué. Straight stitching may not be the best choice on fused appliqué in quilts that will be washed because the adhesive may loosen creating a frayed raw edge. Straight stitching is good for wall hangings and is frequently done after layering as part of the quilting: fuse the appliqué in place, layer the project, and stitch the appliqué edges and quilt in one step.

Setup for straight stitching

- Any thread can be used for this stitching. Matching or monofilament invisible thread will blend in with the appliqué. Contrasting and decorative threads will make an outline.

- Use a bobbin thread which matches the top thread for easiest tension and color control.

- If your appliqué has lots of straight lines or large gentle curves, try a special edge-stitch foot. Or, if you are stitching straight lines or gentle curves and quilting in one step, use a walking foot with an open toe. For free-motion straight stitching lower the feed dogs and use a darning foot.

- Make a stitch sample, layered for quilting, and test various stitch lengths to achieve the look you want. The best-size stitch will depend on the size of the appliqué, the fabric, and the thread.

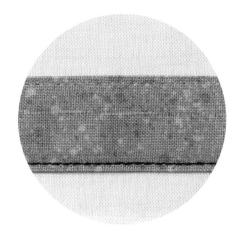

Straight stitching after layering

Special stitching instructions

As you are stitching, maintain an even distance from the appliqué edge. Gauge this with the inside or outside edge of your presser foot and the needle position. Pictured above is the edge-stitch presser foot.

Stitching Corners

Outside Corners

At outside corners and points stop to pivot at the gauged distance from the next edge; continue stitching.

Inside Corners

For inside corners stitch past the corner the gauged distance, pivot and continue stitching.

Outside Corners

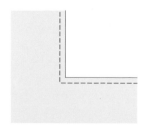

Inside Corners

hand-appliqué stitch

The hand-appliqué stitch is very tiny and almost invisible. It is stitched the same no matter which method of appliqué preparation is used.

Setup for hand appliqué

- The most common threads used for hand appliqué are 60-weight cotton embroidery or silk in a color matching the appliqué.

- Because each person's hands vary, you may need to practice with different needle sizes and types to find the one you like. Start with Sharps size 11. If you like a shorter needle, try Betweens; or longer, try Straw or Milliner's needle. Also try a smaller (12) or larger (10) needle.

- Work with a knotted length of thread about 18" long. This length allows you to make many stitches. A longer thread may become frayed or twisted from too many stitches and can be unwieldy.

Stitching Instructions

Insert the threaded needle from the wrong side directly under the edge of the appliqué. Bring the needle up through the under side of the folded edge of the appliqué just catching one or two threads.

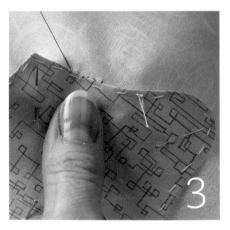

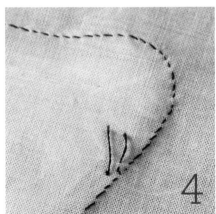

Stitch directly down into the background fabric. Holding the needle parallel to the appliqué edge, bring the point up in the fold of the appliqué about ⅛" from the previous stitch.

Continue stitching around the appliqué giving the thread a gentle tug to firm the stitch, but not so tight to create puckers.

When finished stitching, insert the needle as for another stitch through to the back. Knot.

Hand-stitching knots

A fine but secure knot is essential for hand appliqué. This is the same knot you may already be using for hand quilting.

 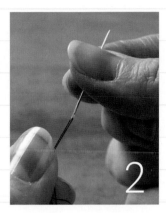 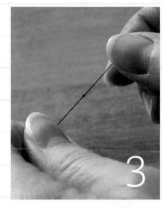 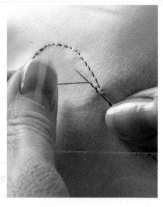

Beginning knot

Position the threaded end of a needle in your right hand, holding it between the thumb and forefinger. Hold about ½" of the end just cut from the spool with the same fingers. Use the other hand to wrap the thread two or three times around the needle.

Grip the wrapped threads with your left hand fingers on the needle. Pull the needle with the right hand and slide the stitches down the needle and to the end of the thread.

You will have a small firm knot.

Ending knot

Take a small stitch in the background under the appliqué. Insert the needle again and wrap the thread around the needle a few times. Pull the needle through. Cut the thread.

Alternate position for hand appliqué

Some appliquérs feel they can see the stitching more easily and that the position of the hands is ergonomically better for the wrists when they work along the bottom edge of an appliqué piece. The stitch is made the same. Try both holding positions.

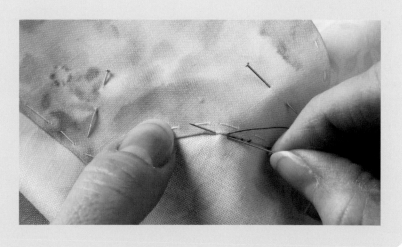

needle-turn hand appliqué

Needle-turn appliqué derives its name from the action of turning under the seam-allowance edge with the needle used for the stitching. The preparation is simple, using either marked line or freezer-paper template for hand-appliqué techniques, page 34.

Setup for needle-turn appliqué

- The most common threads used for hand appliqué are 60-weight cotton embroidery or silk thread in a color matching the appliqué.

- Review the hand appliqué stitch instructions on page 58 for needle choices.

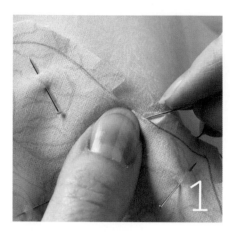

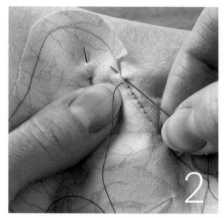

Stitching Instructions

Use the hand-appliqué stitch on page 58. Start on a gentle curve or straight edge. Use the needle to sweep under about 1" of the edge so none of the marked line shows.

Hold seam allowance in place with the tip of your thumb. Insert the needle from the wrong side directly under the edge of the appliqué. Bring the needle up through the under side of the folded edge of the appliqué just catching one or two threads. Continue stitching as directed in steps 2 and 3, page 58.

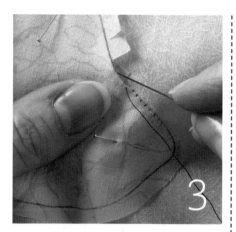

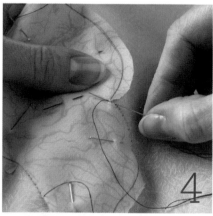

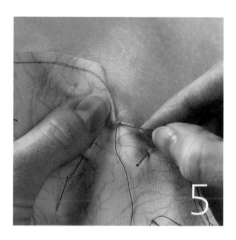

Inside Curves

As you approach an inside curve, clip the seam allowance just to the marked line. Sweep the needle to turn under a small portion of the edge. Take a few stitches and sweep again. For a very tight curve, you will need to make stitches closer together.

Inside Corners

As you approach an inside corner, clip the seam allowance just to the marked line. Make appliqué stitches closer together as you approach the corner. Push any frayed threads under the appliqué. Add one extra stitch to secure the corner.

Sweep under the seam allowance on the other side of the corner and continue stitching.

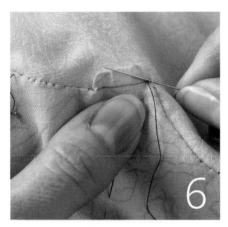

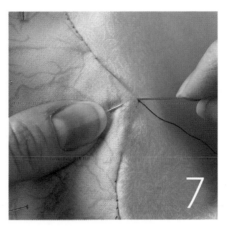

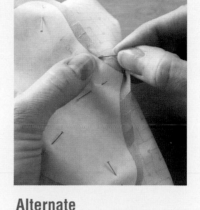

Outside Corner or Point

Stitch to an outside corner with appliqué stitch. Bring the needle up at the point and take one stitch to emphasize the point.

Sweep the seam allowance under on the other side of the point and continue stitching.

notebook

Alternate Freezer-Paper Template

If using a freezer-paper template on top of the appliqué pieces, sweep under the seam allowance even with the freezer paper. Do not catch the paper in the stitching.

Hand blanket stitch

The hand-sewn blanket or buttonhole stitch has been traditionally used on *broidery perse* and Sunbonnet Sue appliqué. This stitch can be used on fused appliqué or any technique where the edge is turned under.

Insert the knotted, threaded, needle from the wrong side at the edge of the appliqué.

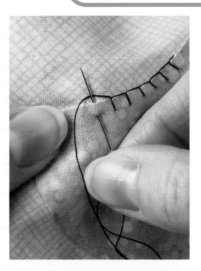

Loop the thread to the left (hold with your left thumb, if desired). Insert the needle through the appliqué about ¼" away from the edge of the fabric and about ³⁄₁₆" left of the first stitch. Holding the needle perpendicular to the edge of the appliqué, bring the point up next to that edge in the background. As you push the needle through, the loop of thread should be under the point. Pull to firm the stitch and repeat, starting with the loop to the left.

tip

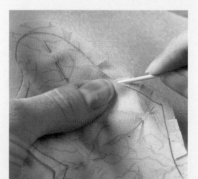

Wooden pick as turning tool

A wooden toothpick can be used instead of the hand sewing needle to turn under the seam allowance.

embellishing

Add special interest to appliqué with embellishing techniques that go beyond basic to beautiful. Let your imagination be your guide as you choose from dozens of decorative stitches, beading, and hand embroidery embellishments shown here and throughout the chapter.

embellishing with programmed stitches

One of the easiest ways to embellish machine appliqué is with the programmed stitches that are on your sewing machine. They can add life-like texture to your appliqué.

Setup for stitching

- A contrasting or decorative thread will show off these decorative stitches.

- Make a sample and test various width and length combinations. The best stitch will depend on the size of the appliqué, the fabric, the thread and the decorative purpose of the stitching.

Stitching Instructions

Each programmed stitch will correlate to one of the basic stitches used to apply appliqué. Refer to the diagrams in *Stitching* for stitching corners and curves.

Use vari-overlock or blind-hem stitches on the edge of leaves that have a prickly texture.

Use a feather stitch on the edge of leaves that have a prickly texture.

A scroll patterned stitch on the upper edge of a tulip petal gives a ruffled feathery look.

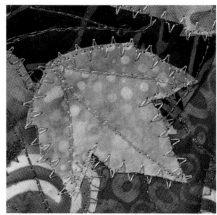

Use programmed multi-zigzag stitch on the edge of leaves that have a prickly texture.

A double-feather stitch in contrasting thread gives added color to the center of this flower.

Programmed stitches

Make a test sample of various stitches programmed on your machine. Mark the test with stitch number.

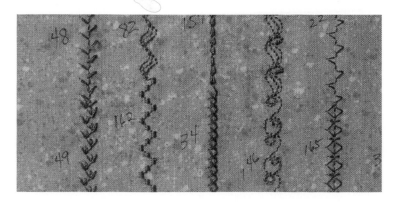

satin zigzag

The satin zigzag stitch is great for adding depth to a flower and to add a contrasting line to any appliqué.

Setup for stitching

- Choose a thread that enhances the appliqué. For the rose, the thread is matching rayon which has a sheen and gives the rolled edge highlights.

Stitching Instructions

Make a sample and test various stitch widths to achieve the look you want. Practice gradually changing the width of the stitch as you are stitching. The best stitch size will depend on the size of the appliqué, the fabric, the thread and the decorative purpose of the stitching.

Follow the stitching Instructions on page 52 for corners, points and curves.

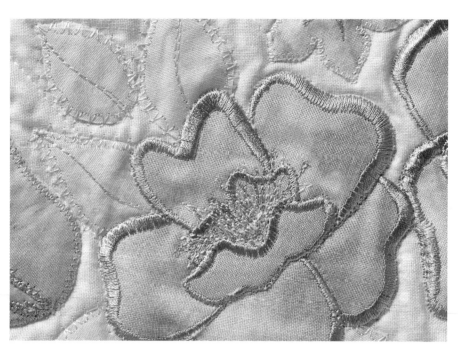

Gradually increase the width of the satin zigzag as you approach the outside edge of each rose petal. Decrease the width as the stitching returns to the center.

Satin zigzag with contrasting thread to help separate two fabrics, enhance the shape of the appliqué piece, or add a line of a different color to embellish the appliqué.

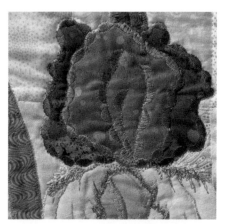

Embellish the edge of a ruffled flower with programmed football-shaped satin zigzag stitches.

Satin zigzag the style and stigma in the center of this rose. These stamens are stitched with free-motion straight stitches.

free-motion zigzag

The free-motion zigzag stitch is great for filling in a broad edge on a flower and giving shading to any appliqué. Free-motion zigzag takes some practice but the decorative element it adds to appliqué and the blending of colors you can get, makes the practice worth it.

Setup for stitching

- Because of the buildup of thread, free-motion zigzag stitching is best stitched on fused appliqué.

- For free-motion zigzag stitching, drop the machine feed dogs and use a darning or free-motion embroidery foot so you can move the appliqué freely.

- Rayon or polyester threads blend better than cotton when using two or more values to shade colors. Cotton 60-weight thread also works well.

- With free-motion zigzag stitching there is a buildup of thread both on the top and the bottom of the appliqué. Use a lighter weight bobbin thread to minimize this, but pay close attention to the tension balance. The top thread should just come through to the back making a very definite "V" shape on the front. You can use a bobbin thread weight that matches the top thread for easiest tension control.

- Set the zigzag stitch at a medium (3 mm) width. Make a sample and test various stitch widths. The best width will depend on the size of the appliqué, the fabric and/or the thread, and if you are trying to replicate a design found in nature.

- Place a piece of removable stabilizer under the appliqué especially when making stitches with a wide zigzag. An embroidery hoop is helpful for extra stability and giving your hands something to hold to guide the fabric.

  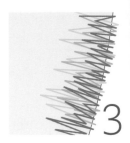

Stitching Instructions

Guide the fabric along the line you are embellishing as the machine moves the needle from side to side. As you guide the fabric also move it from side to side. This will make the stitches an uneven width. (If you just move the fabric slowly in one direction you will get an even width satin zigzag stitch.) Do not try to get full coverage in one forward pass over an area.

1 Stitch about 1" forward.
2 Move back over the same area.
3 Then stitch over the area a third time and move forward to the next area. You can go back over an area later if it needs more coverage or to vary the shape.

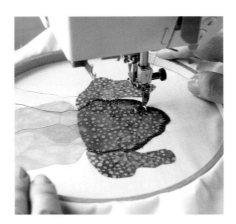

Stabilize for free-motion zigzag stitching

Stabilize for free-motion zigzag stitching with tear away stabilizer under the appliqué pieces and a sturdy embroidery hoop holding the project.

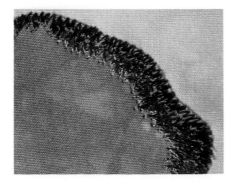

Blending colors

Use free-motion zigzag stitching to shade or blend colors. After stitching the first area (for example the outer edge of this iris petal), change thread to a slightly lighter or darker color value. Stitch again slightly overlapping the stitches so they mesh together.

Single color free-motion zigzag

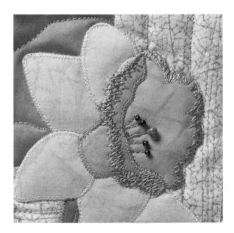

A single shade of orange rayon thread gives a ruffled edge to this daffodil cup. Fine zigzag stitching on the smoother edges of the tulip makes the free-motion orange stitching stand out.

Navy free-motion zigzag stitching marks the dark spots on some oriental poppies. The edges of this poppy are stitched in a single color of red.

Free-motion zigzag stitch the outside edges of the tulip petals with a medium blue thread. Stitch the edges of the inner petals with a lighter shade of blue.

Blended color free-motion zigzag

Bright pink was first free-motion zigzag stitched around these lily petals. A more peach colored thread was then stitched to blend with the first. The stitching broadens and narrows around the petal with fine zigzag stitching where the petal appears to turn under.

Three shades of brown stitched around this iris petal give a ruffled look to the edge. The second and third shades of stitching are broadened where the vein lines will start. The lightest color was free-motion straight stitched for the veins.

The rayon thread colors on this iris petal are light yellow, light blue and medium blue. The free-motion stitching around the edge is the same method as the brown iris at left.

stitching veins and lines

There are several stitches that can be used for lines such as leaf veins, a teddy's mouth, or cat's whiskers. Each stitch gives a different look. Make a stitch sample of each for reference.

Straight Stitch

Sew on the line with a straight stitch using a 30-, 40- or heavier-weight thread. Because backstitching or stitching in place to lock the threads may show, pull thread ends to the back and tie a knot, page 73. Stabilize this type of stitching.

Triple Straight Stitch

The triple straight stitch moves forward, back and then forward again before starting the next stitch, making a heavier line. On curves make all direction changes (even very small ones) by pivoting at the beginning of the sequence. Stabilize this type of stitching.

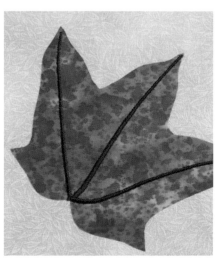

Satin Zigzag Stitch

For a wide line use a satin zigzag stitch. Make samples of different widths to determine what will work best for your project. You can increase or decrease the width of the line as you stitch. Stabilize this type of stitching.

Free-motion Zigzag Stitch

Moving the appliqué sideways, you can stitch a straight or slightly curved line. Use this method for making veins when you are already using the the same set-up for stitching around the edge. Stabilize this type of stitching.

Marking lines for embellishing

There are several ways to mark a line for stitching. Choose the best one for your project.

A line can be marked with a pencil, removable marker, or chalk, page 18, directly on the appliqué. Stitch on the line, using stabilizer on the back.

Trace or draw the line you want to stitch on tracing or tissue paper or tear-away stabilizer with a permanent marker or pencil. Place in position on the appliqué. Stitch on the line. Tear away the paper. You can place tissue or stabilizer you can see through on your pattern to trace the lines, if desired. An advantage of this method is that you do not have to use additional stabilizer.

You do not have to mark the lines if you feel comfortable making straight lines or easy curves as you stitch. The variety you will achieve will be very realistic.

free-motion straight stitching

Free-motion straight stitching is very versatile and is used for leaf veins, flower centers, circles and edge stitching. It is easy to switch from free-motion zigzag stitching to free-motion straight stitching and back as you embellish an appliqué piece.

Stitching Instructions

For free-motion straight stitching drop the machine feed dogs and use a darning or free-motion embroidery foot so you can move the appliqué freely.

Stitch two or three times around each oval and then stitching to the next making the ovals appear as grapes on the bunch.

Stitch free-motion curved lines to make the center of this rose. Use two or three shades of yellow to give added realism.

bobbin work

When you want to stitch with a thread too large to go through the eye of the needle, you can often do the stitching from the back with the large or decorative thread wound on the bobbin. This works well with pearl cotton, heavier metallic threads, twisted threads of more than one variety, and other decorative threads.

Setup for bobbin stitching

- Wind the thread on the bobbin using the bobbin winder or by hand. (Some threads may not slide through the bobbin guide very well.)

- Thread the machine with a matching 50-weight cotton or monofilament invisible thread. Adjust the top tension if necessary to a tighter setting. This will help draw the bobbin thread part way into the fabric. Or, leave the top tension at a normal setting and some of the top thread will show on the right side.

- For bobbin work with straight or programmed stitches, use an open-toe embroidery foot with a wide groove on the under side to accommodate the buildup of thread, even though the buildup is on the underside of the fabric. For free-motion bobbin work use a darning foot with the feed dogs down.

Threads for bobbin work

bobbin work, continued

- The tension on the bobbin case will probably have to be loosened. Loosen the tension by turning the screw to the left. (Before you adjust tension, note where the screw slot was positioned.) Insert the bobbin in the case. Test by stitching a few inches and adjust again as necessary. If your machine has a built-in bobbin case, read the manufacturer's instructions for adjusting bobbin

tension. If you have a second bobbin case, now is the time to use it. For safety, make this bobbin-case adjustment in a plastic bag.

- Make a sample and test various stitches and tension adjustments to achieve the look you want. Other adjustments you may want to make are in stitch length or width.

Stitching Instructions

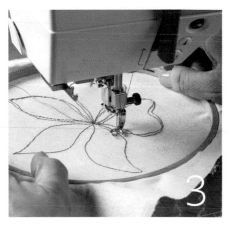

Arrange fused edge appliqué on background. Fuse. Free-motion straight stitch a scant ⅛" inside the edges of the flower petals using a matching thread on the top and a thread that contrasts with the background in the bobbin.

Or, using a turned-edge appliqué method, stitch appliqué with a contrasting thread in the bobbin.

Wind chosen thread on bobbin and make necessary tension adjustments while stitching a test sample.

Place the stitched appliqué in an embroidery hoop. Place the outer hoop on a flat surface; top with the appliqué wrong side up. Insert the inside hoop.

Hold the bobbin and top threads taut as you begin stitching making sure that the bobbin tail does not get caught in the stitching. Using the previous stitching as a guide, free-motion stitch around the appliqué as if you were drawing or sketching the design. Or, use a programmed stitch with the feed dogs up and follow the guide line as desired.

At the end of stitching, leave about a 5" tail on both the top and bobbin threads. Pull the bobbin thread tails through to the back side with a chenille or tapestry needle. Tie in knots. Secure with a small amount of permanent fabric glue.

couching

Couching is a technique used to add yarn or very thick threads to an appliqué or background. For machine couching, a zigzag stitch, other programmed stitch, or free-motion stitching is used to secure a yarn or larger thread to the piece.

Setup for stitching

- For zigzag and decorative stitches use an open-toe embroidery or appliqué presser foot. Or, use a braiding or cording foot to help guide the heavy thread.

- Use invisible monofilament thread, a matching thread, or a contrasting or decorative thread to show off decorative stitches.

- Make a sample to test various stitches and threads. Try standard zigzag, blind hem, serpentine, and various decorative satin stitches.

Threads and yarns to couch

There are a large variety of large threads and yarns that can be couched to appliqué. Several smaller threads can also be twisted together.

Braiding or cording foot

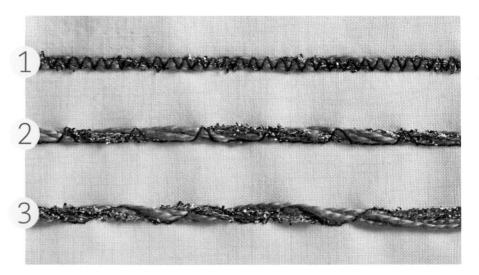

Test sample

Make a test sample of stitches that might work with a yarn.

    Sample 1 Zigzag stitch

    Sample 2 Blind-hem stitch

    Sample 3 Serpentine straight stitch

Evaluate the stitches on how much each one covers the yarn, does it add its own decorative element, and how easy is it to use.

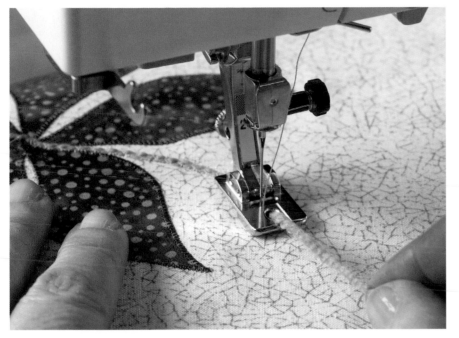

Leave a 5" tail of yarn at end of stitching. Use a chenille or tapestry needle to pull the yarn tail and top thread to the back. Tie a knot with the bobbin thread and secure with a small amount of permanent fabric glue.

Stitching Instructions

Place the appliqué in an embroidery hoop. Place the outer hoop on a flat surface, top with the appliqué right side up. Insert the inside hoop. If you are using a cording or braiding foot, insert yarn to be couched in the hole and pull it through. Leave a 5" tail of the couched yarn when you start stitching. Stitch along the desired line, loosely holding and guiding the couched yarn.

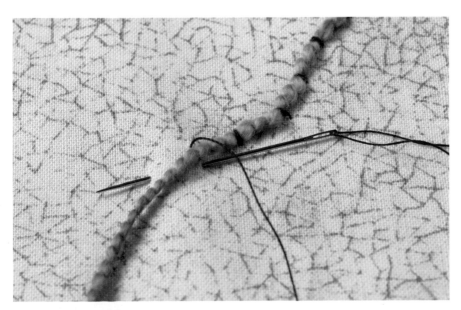

Hand Couching

Stitch a decorative thread or yarn to the quilt top with small stitches about 1/2" apart. Use a matching thread and it will not show. If desired, use a contrasting thread to add more decoration to the couching.

beading

Putting beads, buttons, and other decorations on your finished appliqué adds extra dimension and sparkle to your quilt.

Types of beads

Beads come in glass, plastic, and metal. The glass beads have different finishes: transparent, translucent, opaque, silver or color lined, matte, and satin. Some beads are in shapes, such as hearts, teardrops, flowers, and leaves or have multifaceted sides. Because of the popularity of beading, there are many new shapes and finishes in beads.

Two very common bead types are seed beads and bugle beads. Seed beads are a round squat shape and come in several sizes (14, 11, and 8 are most common with the larger number being smaller). Delicas and magnificas come in similar sizes; they are made by a different method. Bugle beads are long and narrow. They come in sizes 1 to 5 and are sometimes measured in millimeters (5 mm). Bugle beads have very sharp ends because they have been cut.

Buttons and charms can be added to your finished quilt using the same knotting and stitching techniques as for beading. Hide your knots by traveling between the layers.

An assortment of beads

Threads for beading

Specialty beading threads come in waxed and unwaxed and are often made of nylon. Waxed thread can prevent some tangles. Regular 50- or 40-weight cotton thread can also be used. Use a neutral color (gray, taupe, or buckskin) or a color to match beads or the quilt.

Needles for beading

#10 or #12 Betweens or Sharps will go through all of the beads discussed above. Beading needles are about 2" long and when working through layered or quilted appliqué the longer needle may bend.

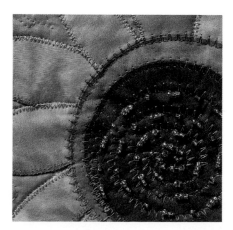

An assortment of yellow beads are spiraled into the center of this sunflower.

Two sizes of beads are used to secure a sequin to the edge of this flower.

This tiger lily is embellished with bugle beads for the tops of the stamen and seed beads for the tiger spots.

Basic beading technique

Although you can add beads to appliqué before it is layered, thus hiding any stitching, it may be difficult to machine quilt around the beads. Below is a technique for adding beads similar to hand quilting.

Work with a knotted length of thread about 18" long, page 59. Insert the needle from the front, bring it to the surface where you want to add the first bead, and pull the knot into the layers as you do when hand quilting.

Place a bead on the needle. At the width of the bead or beads, insert needle into the layers and move to the next position.

To secure as you go, make a small backstitch or knot every 3 or 4 beads or groups of beads. (If thread breaks, you will only lose a few beads.)

End the beading with a knot as for hand quilting by making the knot and pulling it into the layers. Clip the thread.

Specialty Beading

For bugle beads that have sharp cut ends, add a seed bead at both ends or pass the thread through the bugle bead twice.

For larger beads that you want to lay flat, add a seed bead on top and pass the thread back through the larger bead.

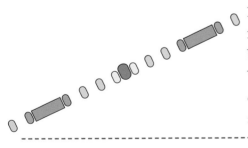

For decorative lines of beads, repeat the same grouping of beads (i.e., 3 seed beads or seed-bugle-seed) at regular intervals, or intersperse sets of beads with single beads.

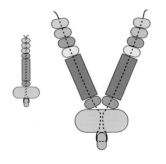

For dangles of beads, thread several beads onto the thread, adding a larger bead or charm in the center. Bring the thread up to the starting point and secure with a knot.

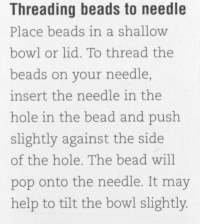

tip

Threading beads to needle

Place beads in a shallow bowl or lid. To thread the beads on your needle, insert the needle in the hole in the bead and push slightly against the side of the hole. The bead will pop onto the needle. It may help to tilt the bowl slightly.

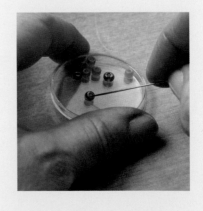

hand embroidery

It seems natural to use hand embroidery stitches on hand appliqué. Some of these are similar to machine stitches and can be used for embellishing in the same way.

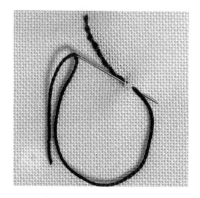

Backstitch

For each stitch move forward the length of two stitches and back one. Insert the needle at the forward end of the last stitch and bring the point up two stitch lengths forward. Repeat.

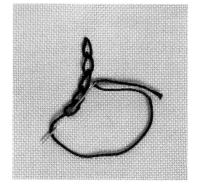

Chain stitch

Form a U shape with the thread and insert the needle back into the same hole. Bring the point up about ¼" forward, catching the loop under the new stitch. Continue making loops.

Feather stitch

Form V shapes for each stitch. Insert the needle about ½" right of the start and bring the point up ½" lower and centered in the V shape. Start a new feather to the left.

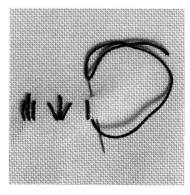

Long stitch

Form stitches that are ½" or longer. Make them in patterns or as running stitches in a line.

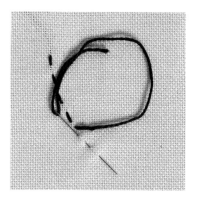

Running stitch

Make forward stitches about ¼" long and ¼" apart. Vary the length of the stitch and the distance between them as desired.

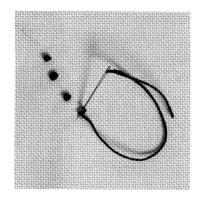

French knots

Bring the needle up at the spot for the knot. Place the point near the fabric and wrap the thread around the needle two or three times. Insert the point into the fabric, very close to the start. Gently pull the needle and thread through the wrapped thread and fabric.

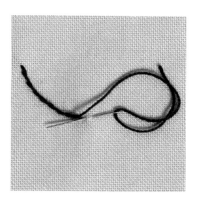

Stem stitch

For each stitch move forward one stitch, inserting and needle and moving back ½ stitch. Keep all of the stitches on the same line.

Step-by-step embellishing
Refer to photographs and flowers from your garden to get embellishing ideas.

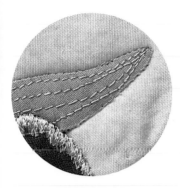

Stitch the leaves and stems
Using a matching rayon thread, free-motion straight stitch the edges of the stems and edges and veins of the leaves.

Stitch the edges of the petals
Using a contrasting thread, free-motion zigzag the edges of the flower petals. Make the stitching broader in some areas to give the petals a rounded appearance.

Stitch the center
Using a decorative color of rayon thread, satin zigzag the center markings on the three upper petals. Start at the center with a wide stitch. As you move away from the center, curve the stitching and gradually narrow the width to a point.

Add beads
Stitch a bugle bead at the end of each stamen. Add a medium bead topped with a seed bead tor the top of the pistil.

Stitch the pistil and stamens
Using a light green rayon thread, free-motion straight stitch slightly curving lines, stitching up and back in the same line.

Tiger spots
Add golden seed beads as if sprinkled on the lily petals.

projects

Be inspired by the featured projects, and then have fun mixing and matching patterns and layouts with the project backgrounds to create your own machine or hand appliqué mini-masterpieces.

clematis treasure

finished size: 10" x 12"

These little treasures are a great way to experiment with different techniques for appliqué and embellishing on a simple color washed background. For a glamorous effect add glittery beads.

materials

Background, Borders and Binding

⅛ yard light green print
⅛ yard medium green print
⅛ yard dark green print
⅛ yard dark purple print for inner border
¼ yard lavender print for outer border and binding

Appliqué

8" square pieces assorted prints (lavender, green) for flower and leaves

Backing

14" x 16" piece backing fabric

Quilt Batting

14" x 16" piece low-loft batting

Fabric suggestions are 40"–42" wide. Sew all patchwork seams with a ¼" seam allowance.

Cut the Quilt Pieces

From the light green print cut

- 1– 3½" x 8½" background rectangle

From the medium green print cut

- 1– 2½" x 8½" background rectangle

From the dark green print cut

- 1– 1½" x 8½" background rectangle

From the dark purple print cut

- 2– 1" x 6½" inner top and bottom borders
- 2– 1" x 9½" inner side borders

From the lavender print cut

- 2– 2" x 7½" outer top and bottom borders
- 2– 2" x 12½" inner side borders
- 2– 1¾" strips for binding

Assemble the Block Background

Lay out the 3 green background rectangles in increasing value. Join to make the quilt center background.

Prepare the Appliqué Pieces

Following your choice of techniques in *Preparing Appliqué*, make the following appliqué pieces. The patterns are found in *Patterns*, page 115. (This Clematis Treasure was prepared with Turned Edge—Freezer Paper and Glue technique, page 28.)

- 1– Clematis
- 1– Clematis Leaf 5
- 1– Clematis Leaf 6
- 1– Clematis Leaf 7
- 1– Clematis Leaf 8

Stitch the Appliqué

1. Arrange the appliqué pieces on the pieced background referring to the photograph, the diagram below, and the layout on page 114. (The layout on page 114 can be enlarged and used to arrange appiqué pieces and mark stem placement lines.) Fuse in place.

2. Stitch the appliqué as desired, referring to *Stitching* and *Embellishing* and the following machine stitching suggestions.

- Clematis—Using monofilament thread, stitch edges of the petals and leaves with blind hem stitching, page 56.

- Flower Veins—Using rayon thread, stitch with free-motion straight stitches, page 68.

- Leaf Veins—Using rayon thread, stitch with free-motion straight stitches, page 68.

- Stems—Stabilize before stitching. Using rayon thread, stitch with satin zigzag stitches, page 68.

Assemble the Quilt

1. Sew the dark purple inner top and bottom borders to the quilt center. Sew the dark purple inner side borders to the quilt center.

2. Repeat with lavender outer borders.

Finish the Quilt

1. Layer the quilt top, batting, and backing.

2. Quilt around the edges of flowers and leaves with invisible thread. Quilt a vine of leaves in the outer border.

3. Trim the excess batting and backing to straighten the edges and square the corners.

4. Bind quilt with the 1¾" lavender print strips, turning binding to the back so the binding does not show on the front.

Using Clematis Treasure and the two examples here for inspiration, play with your favorite patterns on this simple background. These small quilts are great for experimenting with new appliqué preparation and stitching techniques. Use fabric from your stash to try different background gradations, border combinations, and flower colors.

Daylily Treasure

1. Referring to this illustration and the layout on page 117, prepare the appliqué pieces using your choice of techniques in *Preparing Appliqué*.

2. Arrange the appliqué pieces on the pieced background.

3. Stitch the appliqué as desired, referring to *Stitching* and *Embellishing* and the following suggestions.

- Day Lily—Using rayon thread, stitch edges of the under petals with satin zigzag stitches, page 52. Stitch the upper petals with programmed football shaped satin zigzag stitches, page 53.

- Leaves—Using rayon thread, stitch the edges with fine zigzag stitches, page 50, and triple stitch the veins down the middle of each leaf, page 68.

- Centers—Using rayon thread, free-motion straight stitch the stamens, page 70.

On the Vine Treasure

1. Referring to this illustration and the layout on page 119, prepare the appliqué pieces using your choice of techniques in *Preparing Appliqué*.

2. Arrange the appliqué pieces on the pieced background.

3. Stitch the appliqué as desired, referring to *Stitching* and *Embellishing* and the following suggestions.

- Grape Bunch—Using rayon thread and free-motion straight stitching, page 70, stitch ovals about ½" long, stitching two or three times around each oval and then stitching to the next making the ovals appear as grapes on the bunch.

- Leaves—Using rayon thread, stitch the edges with a programmed multi-zigzag stitch, page 64. Free-motion straight stitch the veins, page 68.

- Stems—Stabilize before stitching. Using rayon thread, stitch with satin zigzag stitches, page 68. Refer to page 69 for marking the curly vine.

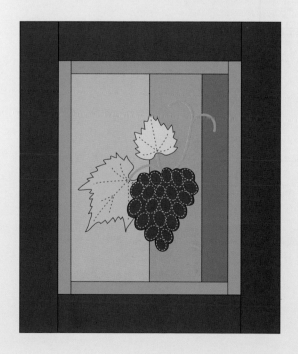

portrait of a daylily

finished size: 18" x 24"

Make a portrait quilt of your favorite flower that will bloom in any room.

materials

Background, Borders and Binding

⅜ yard light green print for background and border corners

⅛ yard dark green print for inner border

½ yard coordinating print for outer border and binding

Appliqué

12" square piece of yellow solid for flowers and buds

14" square piece of bright green print for leaves

12" square piece of yellow-green print for stems

Paper-Backed Fusible Web

1 yard

Backing

22" x 28" piece backing fabric

Quilt Batting

22" x 28" piece low-loft batting

Fabric suggestions are 40"–42" wide. Sew all patchwork seams with a ¼" seam allowance. Follow manufacturer's directions for using paper-backed fusible web.

Cut the Quilt Pieces

From the light green print cut

- 1– 11½" x 17½" background rectangle
- 4– 1½" inner border corner squares

From the dark green print cut

- 2– 1½" x 17½" inner side borders
- 2– 1½" x 11½" inner top and bottom borders

From the coordinating print cut

- 2– 3" x 19½" outer side borders
- 2– 3" x 18½" outer top and bottom borders
- 3– 1¾" strips for binding

Prepare the Appliqué Pieces

1. Referring to *Preparing Appliqué*, page 24, make the following appliqué pieces. The patterns are found in *Patterns*, page 117.

- 2– Daylily 1
- 1– Daylily 2
- 2– Daylily Bud 1
- 2– Daylily Bud 2

2. Refer to the Notebook—Arrange Paper-Backed Fusible Web Appliqué on page 44 to construct flowers and buds.
3. To make stems, apply a 2" x 11" piece of paper-backed fusible web to a bias edge of yellow-green print. Using the instructions for Bias Stems on page 38 in *Preparing Appliqué*, cut 5– ¼" bias stems.

4. To make Daylily leaves, apply a 8" x 12" piece of paper-backed fusible web to a bias edge of bright green print. Using the instructions for bias stems, cut 9– ¾"-wide strips. With rotary cutter or scissors, taper the ends of leaves following the pattern on page 117.

Stitch the Appliqué

1. Arrange the appliqué pieces on the background referring to the photograph, diagram below, and the layout on page 117. (The layout can be enlarged and used to arrange appliqué pieces and mark stem placement lines.)

2. To arrange stem and leaves, position the top or point and lightly press down the length curving into place as you press. The stems and some leaves are positioned behind the lilies. Fuse in place.

3. Stitch the appliqué as desired, referring to *Stitching* and *Embellishing* and the following machine stitching suggestions.

- Leaves and Stems—Using rayon or cotton thread, stitch the edges with fine zigzag stitches, page 50, and triple stitch the leaf veins down the middle of each leaf, page 68.

- Daylilies—Using rayon thread, stitch edges of the 3 under petals and base with fine zigzag stitches, page 50. Stabilize before stitching the 3 upper petals with free-motion zigzag stitches, page 66. Stitch the veins, and stamens with free-motion straight stitches, page 70. Use 2 or 3 shades of thread to emphasize the design.

- Daylily Buds—Using rayon or cotton thread, stitch the edges with fine zigzag stitches.

Assemble the Quilt

1. Sew dark green borders to sides of the quilt center. Sew 1 light green border corner to each end of 2 dark green borders to make top and bottom borders. Sew top and bottom borders to the quilt center.

2. Sew outer side borders to quilt center. Sew outer top and bottom borders to quilt center.

Finish the Quilt

1. Layer the quilt top, batting, and backing.
2. Quilt around the edges of daylilies and leaves with invisible thread. Stitch in the ditch around block borders. Quilt a feather design in the outer border.
3. Trim the excess batting and backing to straighten the edges and square the corners.
4. Bind quilt with the 1¾" print strips, turning binding to the back so the binding does not show on the front.

Imagine your favorite flowers appliquéd in vibrant batik colors. Flip through a few garden catalogs for inspiration and then take your pick from the flowers and layouts in *Patterns.*

Iris Portrait

1. Referring to this illustration and the layout on page 138, prepare the appliqué pieces using your choice of techniques in *Preparing Appliqué*. Make multiple leaves, reversing some, and make several longer than the patterns.
2. Arrange the appliqué pieces on the background.
3. Stitch the appliqué as desired, referring to *Stitching* and *Embellishing* and the following suggestions.

- Iris—Using rayon thread, stitch edges of the upper petals with fine zigzag stitches, page 50. Stabilize before stitching the lower petals and beard with free-motion zigzag stitches, page 66. Stitch the veins with free-motion straight stitches, page 68. Use 2 or 3 shades of thread to emphasize the design.
- Leaves and Stems—Using rayon or cotton thread, stitch the edges with fine zigzag stitches, page 50, and triple straight stitch the veins down the middle of each leaf, page 68.

Tulip Portrait

1. Referring to this illustration and the layout on page 132, prepare the appliqué pieces using your choice of techniques in *Preparing Appliqué*.
2. Arrange the appliqué pieces on the pieced background.
3. Stitch the appliqué as desired, referring to *Stitching* and *Embellishing* and the following suggestions.

- Tulips—Using rayon or cotton thread, stitch edges of the petals with fine or satin zigzag stitches, pages 50 and 52, or stitches featured on the pattern page.
- Leaves and Stems—Using rayon or cotton thread, stitch the edges with fine zigzag stitches, page 50, and triple straight stitch the veins on each leaf, page 68.

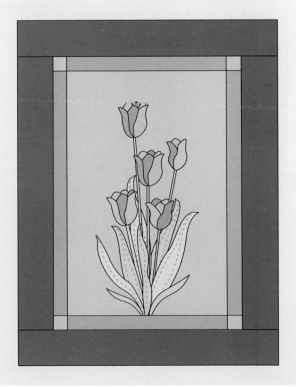

shadow boxes

finished size: 28" x 45"

Appliqué motifs cut from a slightly darker shade of the background fabric give the illusion that these leaves are suspended in air.

materials

Background, Sashing, Borders, and Binding
1 yard light beige print for block background
⅜ yard teal print for block borders and binding
½ yard purple print for block borders and outer border

Appliqué
¼ yard taupe print for shadows
12" square pieces assorted prints (green, gold, brown, rust) for leaves

Paper-backed Fusible Web
1 yard

Backing
1¾ yard backing fabric

Quilt Batting
34" x 51" piece quilt batting

Fabric suggestions are 40"–42" wide. Sew all patchwork seams with a ¼" seam allowance. Follow manufacturer's directions for using paper-backed fusible web.

Cut the Quilt Pieces

From the light beige print cut
- 6– 7½" x 9½" block background rectangles
- 3– 1¾" x 12" vertical sashing rectangles
- 2– 1¾" x 20¾" horizontal sashing rectangles
- 2– 3" x 37½" inner side borders
- 2– 3" x 25¾" inner top and bottom borders

From the teal print cut
- 6– 1¾" x 9½" side block border rectangles
- 6– 1¾" x 10" top and bottom block border rectangles
- 4– 2¼" strips for binding

From the purple print cut
- 6– 1¾" x 9½" side block border rectangles
- 6– 1¾" x 10" top and bottom block border rectangles
- 3– 1¾"-wide strips. Join strips, then cut 2– 1¾" x 42½" outer side borders
- 2– 1¾" x 28¼" outer top and bottom borders

Prepare the Appliqué Pieces

Following the instructions in *Preparing Appliqué*, make the following appliqué pieces. The patterns are found in Patterns, pages 119—127. Make one of each leaf from the "leaf" fabric and one of each leaf from the "shadow" fabric.

- Grape Leaves 1 and 2
- Gingko Leaves 3, 4, and 6
- Sunflower Leaf 1
- Vinca Leaf A (make 3)
- Vinca Leaf B (make 2)
- Vinca Leaf C
- Oak Leaf 4
- Acorn (make 2)
- Maple Leaves 4 and 7

Stitch the Appliqué

1. Arrange the appliqué pieces on the block background referring to the photograph, the diagrams below, and the layouts on pages 118—126. (The layouts can be enlarged and used to arrange appliqué pieces and mark stem placement lines.) Fuse in place.

Grape

Gingko

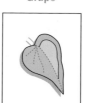
Sunflower

Vinca

Oak

Maple

2. Stitch the appliqué as desired, referring to *Stitching* and *Embellishing* and the following machine stitching suggestions.

- Grape Leaves Block—Using rayon thread, stitch the leaf edges with a programmed multi-zigzag stitch, page 64. Free-motion straight stitch the veins, page 68. Stabilize before stitching the stems with satin zigzag stitches, page 68. Refer to page 69 for marking the curly vine.

- Ginkgo Leaves Block—Using rayon thread, stitch the leaf edges with a free-motion zigzag, page 66, or fine zigzag, page 50. Free-motion straight stitch the veins, page 68. Stabilize before stitching the stems with satin zigzag stitches, page 68.

- Sunflower Leaf Block—Using rayon thread, stitch the leaf edges with a programmed feather stitch, page 64. Free-motion straight stitch the veins, page 68. Stabilize before stitching the stem with satin zigzag stitches, page 68, and if desired, couch a thin yarn for the center vein and stem, page 72.

- Vinca Stem Block—Using rayon thread, stitch the leaf edges with a fine zigzag stitch, page 50. Free-motion straight stitch the veins, page 68. Stabilize before stitching the stem with satin zigzag stitches, page 68. Refer to page 69 for marking the stem.

- Oak Leaf Block—Using rayon thread, stitch the leaf edges with a fine zigzag stitch, page 50. Free-motion straight stitch the veins, page 68. Stabilize before stitching the stem with satin zigzag stitches, page 68.

- Maple Leaves Block—Using rayon thread, stitch the leaf edges and veins with a free-motion straight stitch, page 68. Stabilize before stitching the stem with satin zigzag stitches, page 68.

Assemble the Blocks

1. Sew a teal block border rectangle to each side of a light beige block background; add teal top and bottom block borders.

2. Repeat to make 3 blocks bordered with teal and 3 blocks bordered with purple.

Assemble the Quilt

1. Lay out the appliquéd blocks and the vertical sashing strips in three horizontal rows. Join into rows.

2. Lay out the rows and the horizontal sashing strips. Join to make the quilt center.

3. Sew the light beige inner side borders to the quilt center. Sew the light beige inner top and bottom borders to the quilt center.

4. Repeat with the purple outer borders.

Finish the Quilt

1. Cut the backing fabric into 2– ⅞ yard lengths. Join lengthwise. Seam will run horizontally on the quilt back.

2. Layer the quilt top, batting, and backing.

3. Quilt around the edges of stems and leaves with invisible thread. Stitch in the ditch around block borders and outer borders. Fill the block backgrounds, sashing, and inner borders with a quilted grid or all over design.

4. Trim the excess batting and backing to straighten the edges and square the corners.

5. Use the 2¼" teal strips to bind the quilt.

Choose to make this leaf shadow quilt in a monochromatic color scheme or use the picture frame layout to border a variety of garden flowers. Another idea—choose your favorite flower and make it in several different colors.

Delft Leaves

1. Referring to this illustration and the directions and layouts on page 89, prepare the appliqué pieces using your choice of techniques in *Preparing Appliqué*.
2. Arrange the appliqué pieces on the backgrounds.
3. Stitch the appliqué as desired, referring to *Stitching* and *Embellishing* and the suggestions on page 90.

Framed Flowers

1. Referring to this illustration and the layouts on respective pattern pages, prepare the appliqué pieces using your choice of techniques in *Preparing Appliqué*.
2. Arrange the appliqué pieces on the backgrounds.
3. Stitch the appliqué as desired, referring to *Stitching* and the following suggestions.

• Flowers, Leaves, and Stems—Using rayon or cotton thread stitch the edges of all the pieces with fine zigzag stitches, page 50. Stitch the flower and leaf veins, with free-motion straight stitches, page 68.

• Embellishing—Refer to the ideas on the respective pattern pages and in *Embellishing*.

wind blown

finished size: 19" x 27"

Piece a quietly moving background that enhances the appearance of the wind drifting colorful leaves. Arrange the blowing leaves against a sturdy tree.

materials

Background, Borders, and Binding

1½ yards total of assorted light prints for pieced background

¼ yard medium green print for borders

¼ yard dark green print for binding

Appliqué

10– 9" squares of assorted prints for leaves (golden yellow, orange, rust, brown, burgundy, green)

¼ yard dark taupe print for tree trunk

¼ yard medium taupe print for tree bark highlights

Paper-backed Fusible Web

1½ yards

Backing

⅞ yard backing fabric

Quilt Batting

23" x 34" piece low-loft batting

Fabric suggestions are 40"–42" wide. Sew all patchwork seams with a ¼" seam allowance. Follow manufacturer's directions for using paper-backed fusible web.

Cut the Quilt Pieces

From the assorted light prints cut

- 20 to 26– 1¼" to 2½" x 30" strips for pieced background. The total number of strips needed will depend on the widths cut.

From the medium green print cut

- 1– 1½" x 27" side border
- 1– 1½" x 18" bottom border

From the dark green print cut

- 3– 2¼" strips for binding

Piece the Background

1. Join the assorted light print strips in random order, offsetting each strip approximately ¾". Use the wrong side of some printed strips for very gradual value changes. Continue adding strips until the pieced width is at least 28".

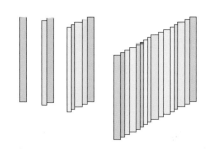

2. Cut the bottom edge at a 30° angle to the seams. Add the resulting triangle to top edge.

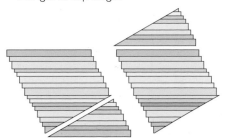

3. Square up the background rectangle to 18" x 26".

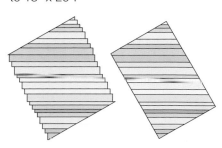

Prepare the Appliqué Pieces

1. Following the instructions in Preparing Appliqué, make the following appliqué pieces. The patterns are found in Patterns, page 127.
   - 10– Maple Leaf 1
   - 10– Maple Leaf 2
   - 5– Maple Leaf 3
   - 5– Maple Leaf 4
   - 10– Maple Leaf 5
   - 5– Maple Leaf 6
   - 5– Maple Leaf 7

2. Cut a 7½" x 26" rectangle of dark taupe print for the tree trunk. Cut gentle curves along both long sides with a rotary cutter. Start at the bottom edge and gradually taper the tree trunk to about 6½" wide at the top.

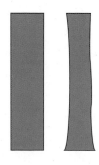

3. Apply a 5" x 16" piece of fusible web to the back of the medium taupe print fabric. Freehand cut tree bark highlights.

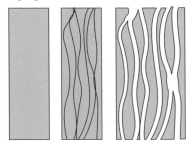

Stitch the Appliqué

1. Pin the tree trunk to the pieced background about 1½" from the lower right edge. Using matching thread, stitch tree trunk edges with fine zigzag stitches, page 50.

2. Arrange the tree bark highlights on the tree trunk. Fuse in place. Using rayon or cotton thread, stitch edges of the bark with free-motion straight stitches, page 70. Using varying shades of rayon or cotton thread, stitch gently-waving lines in the trunk and bark with straight or triple straight stitches, page 68, echoing the curves of the bark highlights.

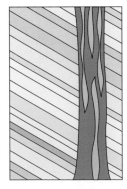

3. Arrange the leaves on the pieced background referring to the

photograph and the diagram below. Save a few leaves to apply after the borders are added. Fuse in place.

4. Trim leaves that overhang the edges of the pieced center. Stitch the appliqué as desired, referring to *Stitching* and *Embellishing* and the following suggestions.

- Maple Leaves 1 through 5—Using rayon thread, stitch the leaf edges with programmed stitches, page 64. Free-motion straight stitch the veins. Stabilize before stitching leaves that are on the sky background.

- Maple Leaves 6 and 7—Using rayon thread, free-motion straight stitch the edges and veins, page 70. Stabilize before stitching leaves that are on the sky background.

Assemble the Quilt

1. Sew the bottom border to the quilt center. Sew the side border to the left edge of the quilt center.

2. Arrange, fuse, and stitch remaining leaves, referring to suggestions in Stitch the Appliqué.

Finish the Quilt

1. Layer the quilt top, batting, and backing.

2. Quilt around the edges of the trunk and leaves with invisible thread. Emphasize the diagonal piecing in the background with freehand loops and swirls.

3. Trim the excess batting and backing to straighten the edges and square the corners.

4. Use the 2¼" dark green strips to bind the quilt.

Imagine this sturdy tree is in the middle of a meadow. It can be the trellis for a vining flower or a canopy for spring flowering bulbs. Your choice—wild roses or wind blown oak leaves?

Summer Trellis

1. Referring to this illustration, prepare the appliqué pieces using your choice of techniques in *Preparing Appliqué*. Reverse some flowers and leaves, if desired.
2. Design a meadow ground under the tree and fuse in place. Arrange the appliqué pieces around the tree.
3. Stitch the appliqué as desired, referring to *Stitching* and *Embellishing* and the following suggestions.
- Clematis, Leaves, and Stems—Using rayon thread, stitch edges of the petals and leaves with fine zigzag stitches, page 50. Stitch the flower and leaf veins, with free-motion straight stitches, page 68. Use 2 or 3 shades of thread to emphasize the petal coloring.

Springtime Meadow

1. Referring to this illustration and the layouts on pages 128 and 130, prepare the appliqué pieces using your choice of techniques in *Preparing Appliqué*. Reverse some flowers and leaves, as desired.
2. Design a meadow ground under the tree and fuse in place. Arrange the appliqué pieces below the tree.
3. Stitch the appliqué as desired, referring to *Stitching* and *Embellishing* and the following suggestions.
- Daffodils and Narcissus—Using rayon thread, stitch the leaf, stem and petal edges with fine zigzag stitches, page 50. Free-motion zigzag stitch the edges of the cups, page 66.
- Muscari—Using rayon thread and free-motion straight stitching, page 70, stitch ovals about ⅜" long, stitching around two or three times and then stitching to the next oval making the ovals appear as bells on the flowers.

spring border

finished size: 22" x 24"

Celebrate spring with this cottage garden border of your favorite spring bulbs.

materials

Background, Borders, and Binding
⅝ yard light blue print for background
¼ yard green print for background
⅛ fuchsia print for inner border
⅝ yard coordinating print for outer border
¼ yard blue print for binding

Appliqué
12" squares of assorted prints for flowers (yellow, golden yellow, pink, rose, white, peach, blue)
⅓ yard blue-green print for stems and daffodil and narcissus leaves
⅛ yard yellow green print for tulip leaves
¼ yard cream print for fence

Paper-Backed Fusible Web
2 yards

Backing
¾ yard backing fabric

Quilt Batting
26" x 28" low-loft quilt batting

Fabric suggestions are 40"–42" wide. Sew all patchwork seams with a ¼" seam allowance. Follow manufacturer's directions for using paper-backed fusible web.

Cut the Quilt Pieces

From the light blue print cut
- 1– 17½" x 19½" background rectangle

From the green print cut
- 1– 17½" x 5" background rectangle

From the fuchsia print cut
- 2– 1" x 17½" inner top and bottom borders
- 2– 1" x 20½" inner side borders

From the coordinating print cut
- 2– 2½" x 18½" outer top and bottom borders
- 2– 2½" x 24½" outer side borders

From the blue print cut
- 3– 2¼" strips for binding

Prepare the Background

1. With right-side up, cut the green print background rectangle on the diagonal from the middle of the left side to the upper corner on the right.

2. Lay the green print background rectangle on top of the blue print background rectangle, matching lower corners.

3. Cut 2– 2" x 20" cream print rectangles for fence rails. Position the lower rail to cover the background overlap. Position the upper rail about 6" above and parallel to the other rail. Pin in place and stitch the edges with fine zigzag stitches in matching thread. Using colors of thread to complement the fence, straight stitch wood grain on the rails. Trim fence rails that overhang the edges of the background.

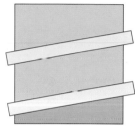

4. Cut 4– 2" x 17" cream print rectangles for fence pickets. Freehand cut points on one end of fence picket rectangles as shown.

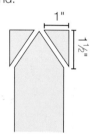

5. Pin the fence pickets on the background. Take care to place the fence pickets straight, parallel and an equal distance apart.

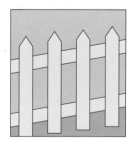

6. Stitch the fence picket edges with fine zigzag stitches in matching thread. Using colors of thread to complement the wood, straight stitch wood grain on the pickets.

Prepare the Appliqué Pieces

1. Following the instructions in *Preparing Appliqué*, make the following appliqué pieces. The patterns are found on pages 129–133 in Patterns. Refer to to the Notebook: Arranging Paper-backed Fusible Web Appliqué, page 44, to construct individual flowers.

- 2– Tulip 3
- 1– Tulip 4
- 2– Tulip 5
- 1– Daffodil 1
- 1– Daffodil 2
- 3– Daffodil Bud
- 1– Narcissus 1
- 2– Narcissus 2
- 7– Muscari 1
- 8– Muscari 2
- 1– Tulip Leaf 1
- 2– Tulip Leaf 2
- 1– Tulip Leaf 3
- 3– Tulip Leaf 4
- 2– Tulip Leaf 5
- 1– Tulip Leaf 6
- 1– Daffodil Leaf 1
- 2– Daffodil Leaf 2
- 2– Daffodil Leaf 3
- 3– Daffodil Leaf 4
- 1– Daffodil Leaf 5
- 1– Narcissus Leaf 1
- 1– Narcissus Leaf 2
- 2– Narcissus Leaf 3

2. Make bias stems using the instructions on page 38 in Preparing Appliqué. Apply a 5" x 13" piece of paper-backed fusible web to a bias edge of blue-green print. Cut 13–¼"-wide strips for stems.

Stitch the Appliqué

1. Arrange the appliqué pieces on the prepared background referring to the photograph, the diagram below, and layouts on pages 128–132. Adjust height of stems and leaves and trim pieces that overhang the edges of the background. Fuse in place.

2. Stitch the appliqué as desired, referring to Stitching and Embellishing and the following machine stitching suggestions.

- Daffodils and Narcissus—Using rayon thread, stitch the leaf, stem and petal edges with fine zigzag stitches, page 50. Free-motion zigzag stitch the edges of the cups, page 66.

- Tulips—Using rayon thread, stitch the leaf and stem edges with fine zigzag stitches, page 50. Stitch the upper petal edges with a programmed scroll stitch, page 64. Free-motion straight stitch the lower edges of the petals and the leaf veins, page 68.

- Muscari—Using rayon thread and free-motion straight stitching, page 70, stitch ovals about ⅜" long,

stitching around two or three times and then stitching to the next oval making the ovals appear as bells on the flower.

Assemble the Quilt

1. Sew the fuchsia inner top and bottom borders to the quilt center. Sew the fuchsia inner side borders to the quilt center.

2. Repeat for print outer borders.

Finish the Quilt

1. Layer the quilt top, batting, and backing.
2. Quilt around the edges of the fence, flowers, and leaves with invisible thread. Quilt in the ditch and with a vine of leaves in the outer border.
3. Trim the excess batting and backing to straighten the edges and square the corners.
4. Use the 2¼" blue strips to bind the quilt. Embellish the daffodil centers with beads.

Create your cottage garden using this rustic picket fence as your background. Play with different groups of flowers, using all of one variety for a mass planting or using several different plants for a more casual feel.

Iris Border

1. Referring to this illustration and the layout on page 138, prepare the appliqué pieces using your choice of techniques in *Preparing Appliqué*. Reverse some flowers and leaves and make several leaves longer than the patterns.
2. Arrange the applique pieces on the background.
3. Stitch the appliqué as desired, referring to Stitching and Embellishing and the following suggestions.

• Iris—Using rayon thread, stitch edges of the upper petals fine zigzag stitches, page 50. Stabilize before stitching the lower petals and beards with free-motion zigzag stitches, page 66. Stitch the veins with free-motion straight stitches, page 68. Use 2 or 3 shades of thread to emphasize the design.

• Leaves and Stems—Using rayon or cotton thread, stitch the edges with fine zigzag stitches, page 50, and triple straight stitch the veins down the middle of each leaf, page 68.

Tiger Lily Border

1. Referring to this illustration and the layout on page 140, prepare the appliqué pieces using your choice of techniques in *Preparing Appliqué*. Reverse some flowers, leaves, and buds.
2. Arrange the appliqué pieces on the background.
3. Stitch the appliqué as desired, referring to Stitching and Embellishing and the following suggestions.

• Tiger Lilies—Using rayon thread, stitch edges of the under petals and buds with fine zigzag stitches, page 50. Stabilize before stitching the upper petals with free-motion zigzag stitches, page 66.

• Leaves and Stems—Using rayon or cotton thread, stitch the edges with fine zigzag stitches, page 50, and free-motion straight stitch the veins, page 68.

100

be mine

finished size: 45" x 45"

Whimsical shapes make this trendy traditional quilt fun to make. Mix and match petals and leaves to make funky flowers.

materials

Background, Borders, and Binding

1 yard white print for block background

¼ yard rose print for block borders

⅝ yard dark green print for block borders and binding

⅓ yard light green check for border corners

¾ yard medium green print for border

Appliqué

10– 9" squares of assorted prints for appliqué shapes (pink, rose, raspberry, turquoise, green)

⅔ yard rose solid for hearts

⅜ yard red print for hearts

Paper Backed Fusible Web

2 yards

Rickrack

180" dusty rose jumbo rickrack

Backing

2¾ yards backing fabric

Quilt Batting

51" x 51" piece quilt batting

> Fabric suggestions are 40"–42" wide. Sew all patchwork seams with a 1/4" seam allowance. Follow manufacturer's directions for using paper-backed fusible web.

Cut the Quilt Pieces

From the white print cut
- 5– 7½" block background squares
- 4– 11½" block background squares

From the rose print cut
- 20– 1½" x 7½" inner block border rectangles

From the dark green print cut
- 20– 1½" x 9½" outer block border rectangles
- 5– 2¼" strips for binding

From the light green check cut
- 40– 1½" squares for block border corners
- 4– 6½" squares for quilt border corners

From the medium green print cut
- 4– 6½" x 33½" borders

Prepare the Appliqué Pieces

1. Following the instructions in *Preparing Appliqué*, make the following appliqué pieces. The patterns are found on pages 125 and 135 in Patterns.

- **Block 1**
  - 1– Petal 3A
  - 2– Petal 1A
  - 2– Petal 1A reversed
  - 1– Leaf 2B
  - 1– Leaf 2A reversed
- **Block 2**
  - 5– Petal 2B
  - 1– Star A
  - 1– Petal 1A
  - 1– Petal 1A reversed

- **Block 3**
  - 1– Scallop C
  - 1– Scallop A
  - 1– Circle B
  - 2– Vinca Leaf C
  - 1– Vinca Leaf B
- **Block 4**
  - 8– Petal 4A
  - 1– Oval A
  - 1– Oval B
  - 2– Petal 2B
  - 2– Petal 2A
- **Block 5**
  - 5– Heart A
  - 1– Circle B
  - 1– Circle A
  - 2– Leaf 1B
- **Border Corner 1**
  - 3– Heart A
  - 1– Oval A
  - 3– Petal 2A
  - 2– Petal 2B
- **Border Corner 2**
  - 8– Petal 4A
  - 1– Circle C
  - 2– Vinca Leaf C
- **Border Corner 3**
  - 5– Petal 5A
  - 1– Scallop A
  - 2– Vinca Leaf C
- **Border Corner 4**
  - 1– Scallop C
  - 1– Circle D
  - 1– Circle B
  - 2– Leaf 2A
  - 1– Leaf 2A reversed
- **Heart Blocks and Borders**
  - 24– Heart C
  - 34– Heart A

2. Make bias stems using the instructions on page 38 in *Preparing Appliqué*. Apply a 2½" x 3½" piece of fusible web to a bias edge of green print. Make 5– 3½" x ¼"-wide strips.

Bordered Blocks

1. Arrange the appliqué pieces on the 7½" white print block backgrounds referring to the photograph and the layouts on pages 104 and 105. (The layouts can be enlarged and used to arrange appliqué pieces and mark stem placement lines.) Fuse in place.

2. Stitch the appliqué as desired, referring to *Stitching* and *Embellishing* and machine stitching suggestions on pages 104 and 105.

3. Sew 1 light green check square to each end of 10 rose print and 10 green print block border rectangles to make top and bottom block borders.

4. Sew rose print inner block border rectangles to sides of background square; add pieced inner top and bottom block borders.

5. Sew dark green outer block border rectangles to sides of bordered white block background; add pieced outer top and bottom block borders.

6. Make 5 bordered blocks.

Heart Blocks

1. Arrange four large and four small hearts on a white print 11½" block background referring to the photograph, the diagram below, the layout on page 134. and Arrange Simple Appliqué, page 42.

2. Machine stitch around the large hearts using a blanket stitch, page 54, and 30-wt. cotton thread. Stitch a fine zigzag stitch, page 50, around the small hearts.

3. Make 4 heart blocks.

Assemble the Quilt

1. Lay out the appliquéd blocks in three horizontal rows. Join into rows. Join rows to make the quilt center.

2. Sew medium green borders to sides of the quilt center. Sew a border corner to each end of 2 medium green borders to make top and bottom borders. Sew top and bottom borders to the quilt.

3. Arrange rickrack on the border, joining lengths at the corners. Attach rickrack by sewing down the middle with a long zigzag stitch.

4. Arrange the appliqué pieces on the corner blocks referring to the photograph and the layouts on page 105. (The layout can be enlarged and used to arrange appliqué pieces.) Fuse in place.

5. Arrange the border hearts and fuse in place.

6. Stitch the corner appliqué as desired, referring to *Stitching* and *Embellishing* and stitching suggestions on page 105. Stitch around the hearts as in the heart blocks.

Finish the Quilt

1. Cut the backing fabric into 2– 1⅜ yard lengths. Join lengthwise.

2. Layer the quilt top, batting, and backing.

3. Quilt around the edges of hearts and appliqué pieces with invisible thread. Stitch in the ditch around block borders. Fill the block backgrounds, and borders with an allover design.

4. Trim the excess batting and backing to straighten the edges and square the corners.

5. Use the 2¼" dark green strips to bind the quilt.

be creative

Want something more traditional than rickrack? Ring this quilt with long lengths of bias stems. Make a sweet rose quilt, play with the funky flower parts to design different flowers, or use a variety of garden blooms in the appliquéd blocks and corners.

Wild Roses Lap Quilt

1. Referring to this illustration, prepare the appliqué pieces using your choice of techniques in *Preparing Appliqué*. Reverse some flowers and leaves.

2. Arrange the appliqué pieces on the backgrounds and follow the instructions for making the various types of blocks.

3. Stitch the appliqué as desired, referring to *Stitching* and *Embellishing* and the ideas on your chosen pattern pages.

funky flowers—layouts and stitching ideas

Mix and match petals and leaves to make funky flowers. Use the photographs below for placement and stitching ideas or make your own whimsical shapes and embellish them using different combinations of stitches.

Copy at 300% for full-size layouts.

Block 1

- Stitch around the leaves and center with a programmed pointed satin stitch, page 64.
- Fine zigzag stitch around the flower petals and stem, page 50.
- Free-motion straight stitch the veins in the leaves and petals, page 68.

Block 2

- Fine zigzag stitch around the center star and stem, page 50.
- Free-motion straight stitch the edges of the petals changing to free-motion circles at the top, page 70.
- Free-motion straight stitch the edges of the leaves, page 70, and an echo line about ¼" inside the edge.

Block 3

- Fine zigzag stitch around the inner flower and stem, page 50.
- Using a contrasting color of rayon thread, satin zigzag stitch around the outer scallop flower, page 52.
- Stitch around the flower center with a programmed pointed satin stitch, and around the leaves with a programmed feather stitch, page 64.
- Free-motion straight stitch the veins in the leaves and petals, page 68.

Block 4

- Straight stitch concentric triangles on the leaves, page 68.
- Fine zigzag stitch around the flower petals and stem, page 50.
- Using a contrasting color of rayon thread, satin zigzag stitch around the two oval flower centers, page 65.

Block 5

- Fine zigzag stitch around the heart petals and stem, page 50.
- Stitch around the larger center circle with a programmed pointed satin stitch, page 64.
- Satin zigzag stitch around the small flower center, page 52.
- Stitch around the leaves with a blanket stitch, page 54.
- Free-motion straight stitch the veins in the leaves, page 68.

Corner Block 1

- Stitch around the center oval with a programmed pointed satin stitch, page 65.
- Fine zigzag stitch around the heart petals and leaves, page 50.
- Free-motion straight stitch the veins in the leaves echoing the edge, page 68.
- Free-motion straight stitch the edges of the petals changing to free-motion circles at the top, page 70.

Corner Block 2

- Stitch around the center with a programmed pointed satin stitch, page 65.
- Fine zigzag stitch around the flower petals, page 50.
- Free-motion straight stitch the petals, page 70.
- Stitch the leaves with a blind-hem stitch, page 64.
- Free-motion straight stitch the veins in the leaves, page 68.

Corner Block 3

- Fine zigzag stitch around the leaves, page 50 and satin zigzag stitch around scallop center, page 52.
- Stitch the petals with a combination of satin zigzag stitches, page 52, and a programmed pointed satin stitch, page 65.
- Free-motion straight stitch the veins in the leaves and the flower center, page 70.

Corner Block 4

- Fine zigzag stitch around the flower scallop and leaves, page 50, and the leaf veins.
- Using a contrasting thread, stitch around the larger circle center with a programmed double feather stitch, page 64.
- Satin zigzag stitch around the small circle center, page 52.

garden chintz

finished size: 42" x 54"

Inspired by an antique English tea pot, this quilt evokes a relaxing party in a country garden. For a completely different look, choose many shades of blue fabric and thread.

materials

Background, Borders, and Binding

¾ yard yellow print for appliqué background

1 yard lavender print for inner border

1½ yards blue print for outer border and binding

⅜ yard green print for border triangles

Appliqué

Fat quarters (18" x 20") of assorted prints for flowers and leaves (golden yellow, white, light and medium rose, light and medium lavender, medium blue, medium green)

Paper-Backed Fusible Web

2 yards

Backing

2½ yards backing fabric

Quilt Batting

48" x 60" quilt batting

Fabric suggestions are 40"–42" wide. Sew all patchwork seams with a ¼" seam allowance. Follow manufacturer's directions for using paper-backed fusible web.

Cut the Quilt Pieces

From the yellow print cut

- 8– 4½" squares. Cut diagonally in both directions to make 32 quarter-square triangles
- 1– 19½" x 31½" background rectangle

From the lavender print cut

- 2– 3½" x 36½" inner side borders
- 2– 3½" x 30½" inner top and bottom borders
- 18– 3⅞" squares. Cut diagonally to make 36 half-square triangles
- 13– 4¼" squares. Cut diagonally in both directions to make 52 quarter-square triangles

From the blue print cut

- 5– 3½"-wide strips. Join strips, then cut 2– 3½" x 48½" outer side borders and 2– 3½" x 42½" outer top and bottom borders
- 26– 3⅞" squares. Cut diagonally to make 52 half-square triangles
- 1– 4¼" square. Cut diagonally in both directions to make 4 quarter-square triangles
- 6– 2¼" strips for binding

From the green print cut

- 22– 4¼" squares. Cut diagonally in both directions to make 88 quarter-square triangles

Prepare the Appliqué Pieces

Following the instructions in *Preparing Appliqué*, make the following appliqué pieces. The patterns are found on pages 131, 133, and 137 in Patterns.

- 2– Rose 1
- 4– Rose 2
- 5– Tulip 3
- 7– Daffodil 3
- 20– Star Flower 1
- 24– Star Flower 2
- 4– Star Petal 1
- 5– Star Petal 2
- 12– Rose Leaf 3
- 24– Rose Leaf 2
- 15– Rose Leaf 1

Stitch the Appliqué

1. Arrange appliqué pieces on the background rectangle referring to the photograph, and the diagrams and the layout on page 109. (The layout can be enlarged and used to arrange appliqué pieces and mark stem placement lines.) Fuse in place.

2. Stitch the appliqué as desired, referring to *Stitching* and *Embellishing* and the following machine stitching suggestions.

- Roses—Using rayon thread, stitch the edges with satin zigzag stitches, page 65, increasing the stitch width along the outside edges of the petals. Stitch centers and stamens with free-motion straight stitches, page 70.

- Daffodils—Using rayon thread, stitch edges of the 5 petals and lower cup with fine zigzag stitches, page 50. Stabilize before stitching the upper edge of the cup with free-motion zigzag stitches, page 66. Use 2 or 3 shades of thread to emphasize the design.

- Tulips—Using rayon thread, stitch the lower edges of the petals with fine zigzag stitches, page 50. Free-motion zigzag stitch the upper edges of the outer petals, page 66, varying the shade of thread on different petals.

- Star Flowers—Using a matching color of rayon thread, stitch the petals with fine zigzag stitches, page 50. Using contrasting thread, free-motion straight stitch the center, page 70.

- Rose Leaves—Stabilize before stitching the leaves. Using rayon thread, blind hem stitch around the edges of each leaf, page 64. Free-motion zigzag stitch the veins, page 68.

3. After the appliqué has been stitched, trim the background to 18½" x 30½".

Make the Pieced Borders

1. Join 1 green and 1 yellow quarter-square triangle with 1 lavender half-square triangle to make Unit A. Make 32.

2. Join 1 green and 1 lavender quarter-square triangle with 1 lavender half-square triangle to make Unit B. Make 4.

3. Join 1 lavender and 1 green quarter-square triangle with 1 blue half-square triangle to make Unit C. Make 48.

4. Join 1 blue and 1 green quarter-square triangle with 1 blue half-square triangle to make Unit D. Make 4.

5. Join 10 Unit A squares to make pieced inner side borders.

6. Join 6 Unit A squares and 2 Unit B squares to make pieced inner top and bottom borders.

7. Join 14 Unit C squares to make pieced outer side borders.

8. Join 10 Unit C squares and 2 Unit D squares to make pieced outer top and bottom borders.

Assemble the Quilt

1. Sew the pieced inner side borders to the quilt center. Sew the pieced inner top and bottom borders to the quilt center.

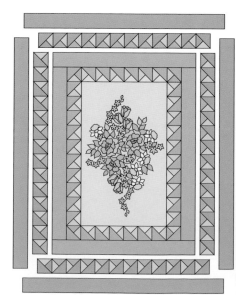

2. Repeat with lavender inner borders, pieced outer borders, and blue outer borders.

3. Arrange, fuse, and stitch the border
appliqué pieces, referring to the corner
layouts on this page and stitching
suggestions in Stitch the Appliqué.

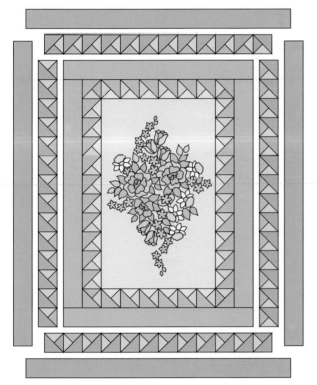

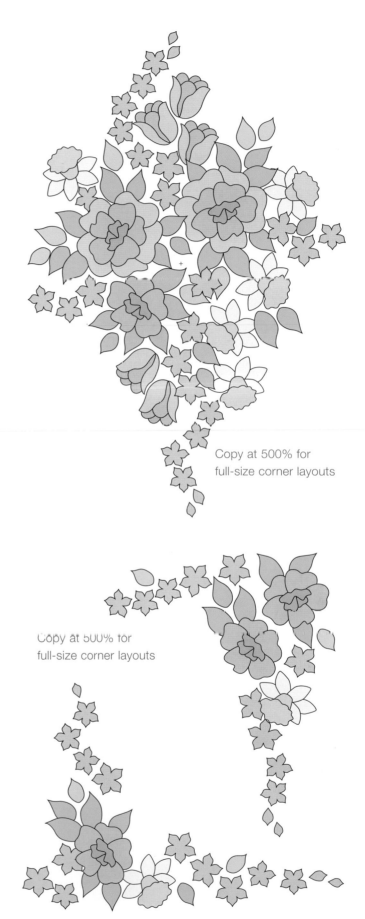

Copy at 500% for
full-size corner layouts

Copy at 500% for
full-size corner layouts

Finish the Quilt

1. Cut the backing fabric into 2– 1¼ yard
lengths. Join lengthwise. Seam will run
horizontally on the quilt back.

2. Layer the quilt top, batting, and
backing.

3. Quilt around the edges of flowers and
leaves with invisible thread. Fill the
center background with a quilted grid,
and quilt a vine of leaves in each
border.

4. Trim the excess batting and backing to
straighten the edges and square the
corners.

5. Use the 2¼" blue strips to bind the quilt.

delft blue chintz

finished size: 42" x 54"

Make Garden Chintz in shades of blue for a quilt reminiscent of Dutch pottery.

materials

Background, Borders, and Binding

¾ yard white print for appliqué background

1 yard light blue print for inner border

1½ yards medium blue print for outer border and binding

⅜ yard dark blue print for border triangles

Appliqué

Fat quarters (18" x 20") of assorted prints for flowers and leaves (light, medium, and dark blue; white)

Paper-Backed Fusible Web

2 yards

Backing

2½ yards backing fabric

Quilt Batting

48" x 60" quilt batting

Fabric suggestions are 40"–42" wide. Sew all patchwork seams with a ¼" seam allowance. Follow manufacturer's directions for using paper-backed fusible web.

Cut the Quilt Pieces

From the white print cut

- 8– 4½" squares. Cut diagonally in both directions to make 32 quarter-square triangles
- 1– 19½" x 31½" background rectangle

From the light blue print cut

- 2– 3½" x 36½" inner side borders
- 2– 3½" x 30½" inner top and bottom borders
- 18– 3⅞" squares. Cut diagonally to make 36 half-square triangles
- 13– 4¼" squares. Cut diagonally in both directions to make 52 quarter-square triangles

From the medium blue print cut

- 5– 3½"-wide strips. Join strips, then cut 2– 3½" x 48½" outer side borders and 2– 3½" x 42½" outer top and bottom borders
- 26– 3⅞" squares. Cut diagonally to make 52 half-square triangles
- 1– 4¼" square. Cut diagonally in both directions to make 4 quarter-square triangles
- 6– 2¼" strips for binding

From the dark blue print cut

- 22– 4¼" squares. Cut diagonally in both directions to make 88 quarter-square triangles

Prepare the Appliqué Pieces

Following the instructions in *Preparing Appliqué*, make the following appliqué pieces. The patterns are found on pages 131, 133, and 137 in Patterns.

- 2– Rose 1
- 1– Rose 2
- 5– Tulip 3
- 5– Daffodil 3
- 9– Star Flower 1
- 13– Star Flower 2
- 2– Star Petal 1
- 2– Star Petal 2
- 7– Rose Leaf 3
- 17– Rose Leaf 2
- 10– Rose Leaf 1

Stitch the Appliqué

1. Arrange the appliqué pieces on the background rectangle referring to the photograph, and the diagrams and layout on page 109. (The layout can be enlarged and used to arrange appliqué pieces.) Fuse in place.
2. Stitch the appliqué as desired, referring to *Stitching* and *Embellishing* and the suggestions on pages 107–108.
3. After the appliqué has been stitched, trim the background to 18½" x 30½".

Make the Pieced Borders

1. Join 1 dark blue and 1 white quarter-square triangle with 1 light blue half-square triangle to make Unit A. Make 32.
2. Join 1 dark blue and 1 light blue quarter-square triangle with 1 light blue half-square triangle to make Unit B. Make 4.
3. Join 1 light blue and 1 dark blue quarter-square triangle with 1 medium blue half-square triangle to make Unit C. Make 48.
4. Join 1 medium blue and 1 dark blue quarter-square triangle with 1 medium blue half-square triangle to make Unit D. Make 4.
5. Join 10 Unit A squares to make pieced inner side borders.
6. Join 6 Unit A squares and 2 Unit B squares to make pieced inner top and bottom borders.
7. Join 14 Unit C squares to make pieced outer side borders.
8. Join 10 Unit C squares and 2 Unit D squares to make pieced outer top and bottom borders.

Assemble the Quilt

1. Sew the pieced inner side borders to the quilt center. Sew the pieced inner top and bottom borders to the quilt center.
2. Repeat with light blue inner borders, pieced outer borders, and medium blue outer borders.

Finish the Quilt

1. Cut the backing fabric into 2– 1¼ yard lengths. Join lengthwise. Seam will run horizontally on the quilt back.
2. Layer the quilt top, batting, and backing.
3. Quilt around the edges of flowers and leaves with invisible thread. Fill the center background with a quilted grid, and quilt a vine of leaves in each border.
4. Trim the excess batting and backing to straighten the edges and square the corners.
5. Use the 2¼" blue strips to bind the quilt.

patterns

Treat yourself to full-size patterns for the featured designs. Each design is accompanied by helpful photographs showcasing stitching and embellishing ideas to make every appliqué your own unique creation.

clematis

Pattern Preparation: The clematis and leaves were prepared with turned edges.

Stitching: Using monofilament invisible thread, stitch the edges with blind hem stitch, page 56. The veins in the leaves and flowers were stitched with a slightly darker thread using straight stitches. Stitch the stems with satin zigzag stitches, page 68.

Embellishing: Free-motion straight stitch curves to simulate the center of the flower, page 70.

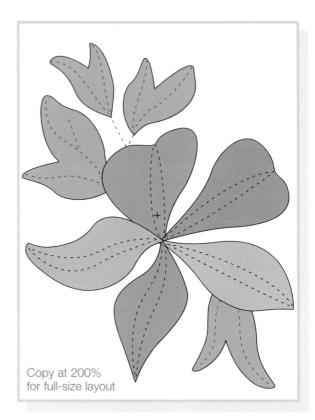

Copy at 200% for full-size layout

Pattern Preparation: The clematis and leaves were prepared with paper-backed fusible web, page 24.

Embellishing: Use bobbin work to stitch the clematis petals, page 70. Stitch the leaves and veins, flower veins, and flower center with free-motion straight stitches, page 70.

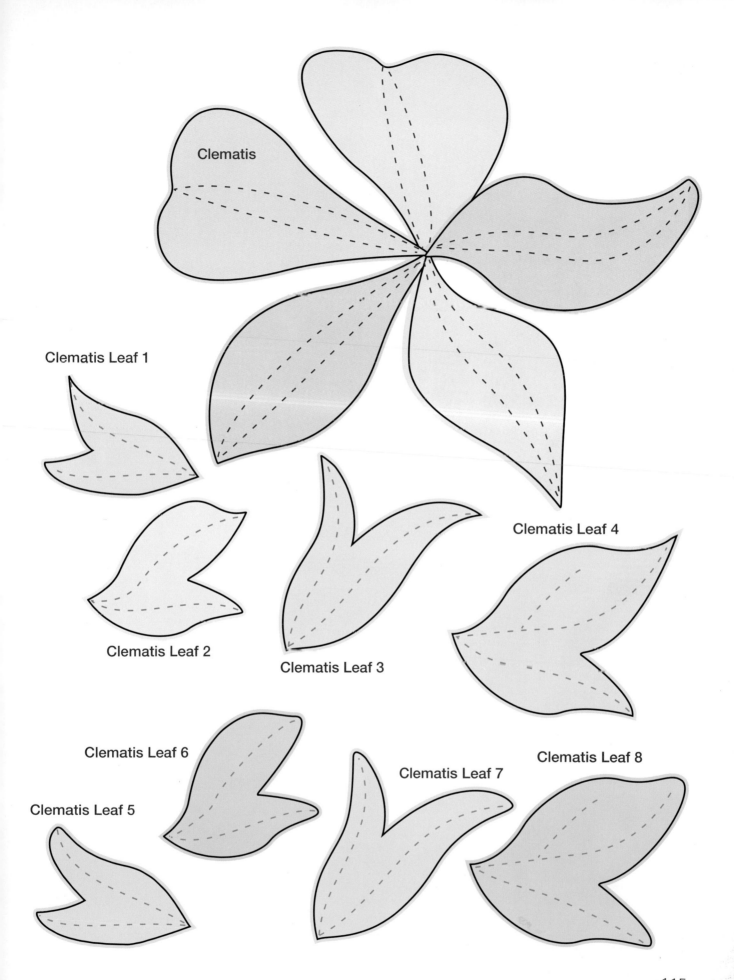

Clematis

Clematis Leaf 1

Clematis Leaf 2

Clematis Leaf 3

Clematis Leaf 4

Clematis Leaf 5

Clematis Leaf 6

Clematis Leaf 7

Clematis Leaf 8

daylily

Pattern Preparation: The daylily flowers and leaves were prepared with paper-backed fusible web, page 24.

Stitching: Using matching colors of rayon thread, fine zigzag istitch around the stems, leaves, and buds, page 50. Straight stitch the veins, page 68.

Embellishing: Free-motion zigzag stitch around the flower petals, page 50. Use a combination of free-motion straight stitching and satin zigzag stitches for the flower center, pages 70 and 65.

Copy at 400% for full-size layout

Pattern Preparation: The daylily flowers and leaves were prepared with paper-backed fusible web, page 24.

Stitching: Using matching colors of rayon thread, fine zigzag istitch around the stems, leaves, and buds, page 50. Straight stitch the veins, page 68.

Embellishing: Free-motion zigzag stitch around the flower petals, page 50. Use a combination of free-motion straight stitching and satin zigzag stitches for the flower center, pages 70 and 65.

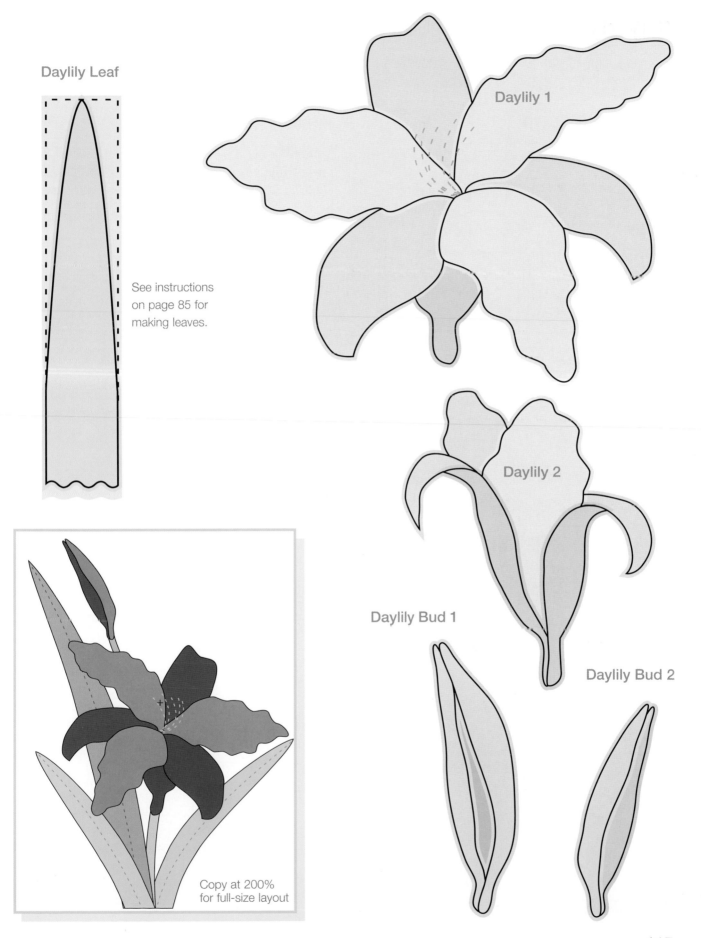

Daylily Leaf

See instructions
on page 85 for
making leaves.

Daylily 1

Daylily 2

Daylily Bud 1

Daylily Bud 2

Copy at 200%
for full-size layout

grape leaves and grape bunches

Pattern Preparation: The grape leaves (1 and 2) were prepared with paper-backed fusible web, page 24.

Stitching: Use a programmed multi-zigzag stitch around the leaves, page 64. Free-motion straight stitch the leaf veins, page 68. Satin zigzag stitch the stem, gradually decreasing the width as you approach the curled tip, page 65.

Copy at 200%
for full-size layout

Pattern Preparation: The grape leaves (1 and 2) and grape bunch were prepared with paper-backed fusible web, page 24.

Stitching: Use a programmed multi-zigzag stitch around the leaves, page 64. Free-motion straight stitch the leaf veins, page 68. Satin zigzag stitch the stem, gradually decreasing the width as you approach the curled tip, page 65.

Embellishing: Using a light thread, free-motion straight stitch ovals to resemble grapes in the grape bunch, page 70, moving in a continuous line from one grape to the next.

Grape Bunch

Single Grape

Copy at 200% for
full-size layout of
individual grapes in
a bunch

Grape Leaf 2

Grape Leaf 3

Grape Leaf 1

Grape Leaf 4

Copy at 200%
for full-size grape
bunch layout

gingko leaves

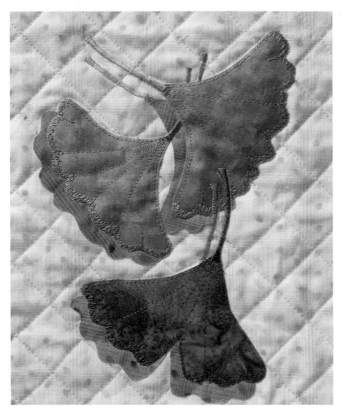

Pattern Preparation: The gingko leaves (3, 4, and 6) were prepared with paper-backed fusible web, page 24.

Embellishing: Free-motion zigzag stitch the lower edges of the gingko leaves, page 66. Free-motion straight stitch the remaining edges and the veins, page 68. Stitch the stem with satin zigzag stitches, page 68. gradually curve and widen the zigzag at the base of the stem to simulate the place where it separates from the branch.

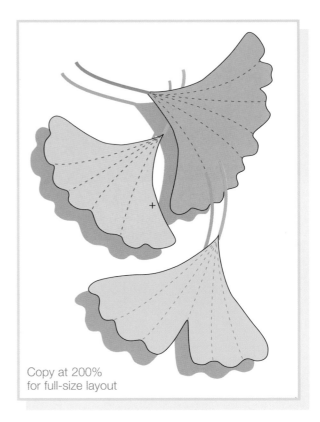

Copy at 200%
for full-size layout

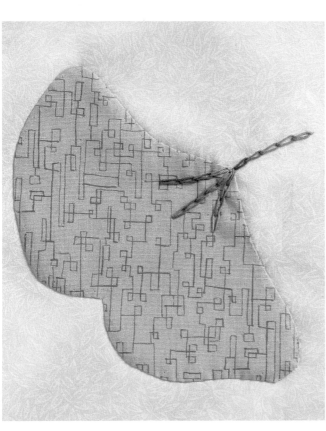

Pattern Preparation: The gingko leaf (1) was prepared with marked line for hand appliqué, page 34.

Stitching: Stitch using needle-turn hand appliqué, page 58.

Embellishing: With variegated 12-wt cotton thread make veins and stem with hand embroidered daisy chain, page 76.

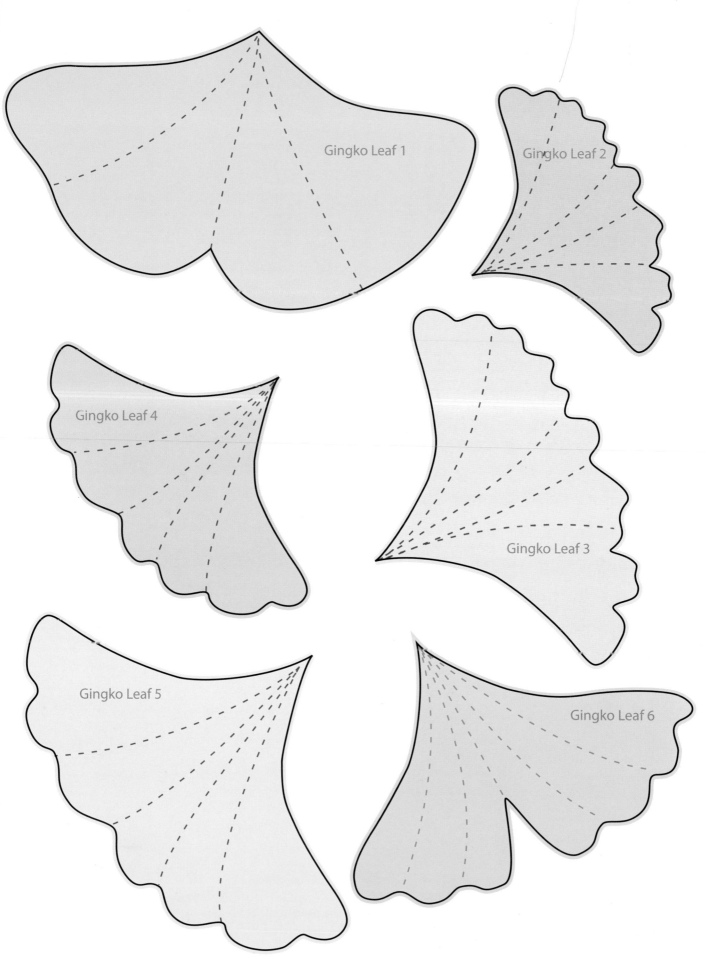

Gingko Leaf 1

Gingko Leaf 2

Gingko Leaf 4

Gingko Leaf 3

Gingko Leaf 5

Gingko Leaf 6

sunflower and leaves

Pattern Preparation: The sunflower leaf (1) was prepared with paper-backed fusible web, page 24, and has reverse appliqué, page 36.

Stitching: Stitch the edges of the leaf with a programmed feather stitch, page 64. Stitch the veins with free-motion straight stitches in a contrasting color, page 68.

Embellishing: Stitch the center vein and stem with satin zigzag stitches starting at the tip of the leaf, page 68. Gradually increase the stitch width as you stitch to the base, adding a yarn to couch about half way to the base of the leaf, page 72.

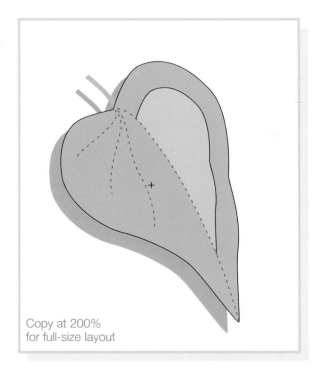

Copy at 200%
for full-size layout

Pattern Preparation: The sunflower was prepared with paper-backed fusible web, page 24.

Stitching: Stitch the edges of the petals with a fine zigzag stitch, page 50. Stitch the edges of the center with a decorative button hole stitch, page 64, spiraling the stitching into the center.

Embellishing: Add a line of seed beads following the spiral of the stitching, page 74.

Sunflower Leaf 1

Sunflower Leaf 2

Petal 1

Petal 2

Petal 3

Sunflower

Sunflower
Petal 3
Alternate

Sunflower
Petal 2
Alternate

Sunflower
Petal 1
Alternate

Copy at 300%
for full-size layout

oak leaves

Pattern Preparation: The oak leaf (4) and acorns were prepared with paper-backed fusible web, page 24.

Stitching: Use a fine zigzag stitch in matching colors of rayon thread around the edges, page 50. Starting at the tip of the leaf, stitch the veins and stem with satin zigzag, page 68. Gradually increase the width as you stitch to the base. As you continue stitching the stem give it a gentle curve. Widen the zigzag to about 4 at the top of the stem to simulate the place where it separates from the branch.

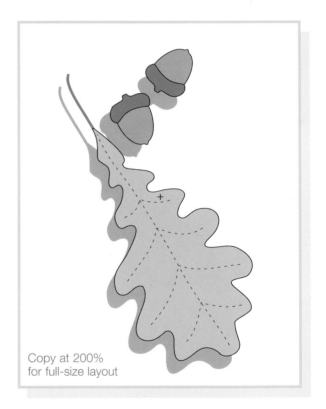

Copy at 200% for full-size layout

Pattern Preparation: The oak leaf (2) was prepared with paper-backed fusible web.

Embellishing: Using a variegated teal medley 12-weight cotton thread blanket stitch the edges of the leaf, page 54. Free-motion straight stitch the veins, page 68.

Oak Leaf 1

Oak Leaf 2

Oak Leaf 3

Oak Leaf 4

Oak Leaf 5

Acorn

Copy at 200%
for full-size layout

D

C

B

A

Vinca Leaves

maple leaves

Pattern Preparation: The maple leaves (7 and 4) were prepared with paper-backed fusible web, page 24.

Stitching: Free-motion straight stitch the edges and veins of the leaves, page 68.

Embellishing: Stitch the stems with a satin zigzag starting at the base of the leaf, page 68. Widen the zigzag at the base of the stem to simulate the place where it separates from the branch.

Copy at 200% for full-size layout

Pattern Preparation: The maple leaf (5) was prepared with paper-backed fusible web, page 24.

Stitching: Use a programmed multi-zigzag stitch around the leaves, page 64. Free-motion straight stitch the leaf veins, page 68.

Maple Leaf 1

Maple Leaf 2

Maple Leaf 3

Maple Leaf 4

Maple Leaf 5

Maple Leaf 6

Maple Leaf 7

daffodils

Pattern Preparation: The daffodil (1) was prepared with paper-backed fusible web, page 24.

Stitching: Using matching colors of rayon thread, fine zigzag stitch around the edges of the lower petals, leaves and stems, page 50.

Embellishing: Free-motion zigzag stitch the outer edges of the daffodil cup, page 66. Free-motion straight stitch pistil and stamens, page 70. After layering and quilting add beads to the center, page 74.

Copy at 400% for full-size layout

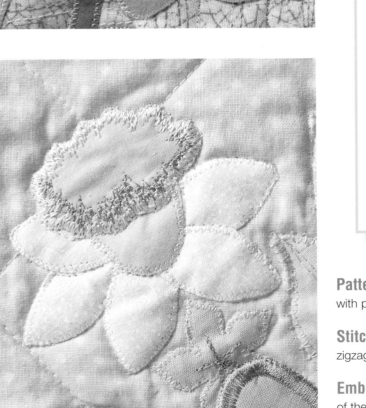

Pattern Preparation: Daffodil 3, page 131 was prepared with paper-backed fusible web, page 24.

Stitching: Using matching colors of rayon thread, fine zigzag stitch around the edges of the lower petals, page 50.

Embellishing: Free-motion zigzag stitch the outer edges of the daffodil cup, page 66.

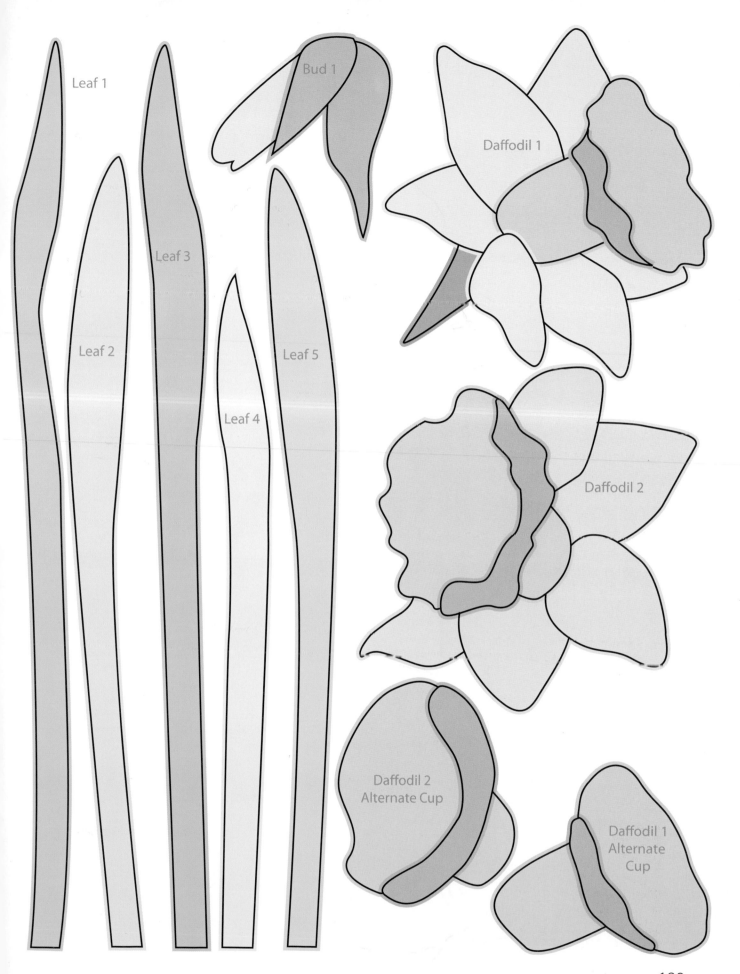

Leaf 1

Leaf 2

Leaf 3

Leaf 4

Leaf 5

Bud 1

Daffodil 1

Daffodil 2

Daffodil 2 Alternate Cup

Daffodil 1 Alternate Cup

129

narcissus and muscari

Pattern Preparation: The narcissus were prepared with paper-backed fusible web, page 24.

Stitching: Using matching colors of rayon thread, fine zigzag stitch around the edges of the lower petals, leaves and stems, page 50.

Embellishing: Free-motion zigzag stitch the outer edges of the daffodil cup, page 66.

Copy at 300% for full-size layout

Pattern Preparation: The muscari were prepared with paperbacked fusible web, page 24.

Embellishing: Using rayon thread and free-motion straight stitching, page 70 stitch ovals about ⅜" long, stitching around two or three times and then stitching to the next oval making the ovals appear as bells on the flower.

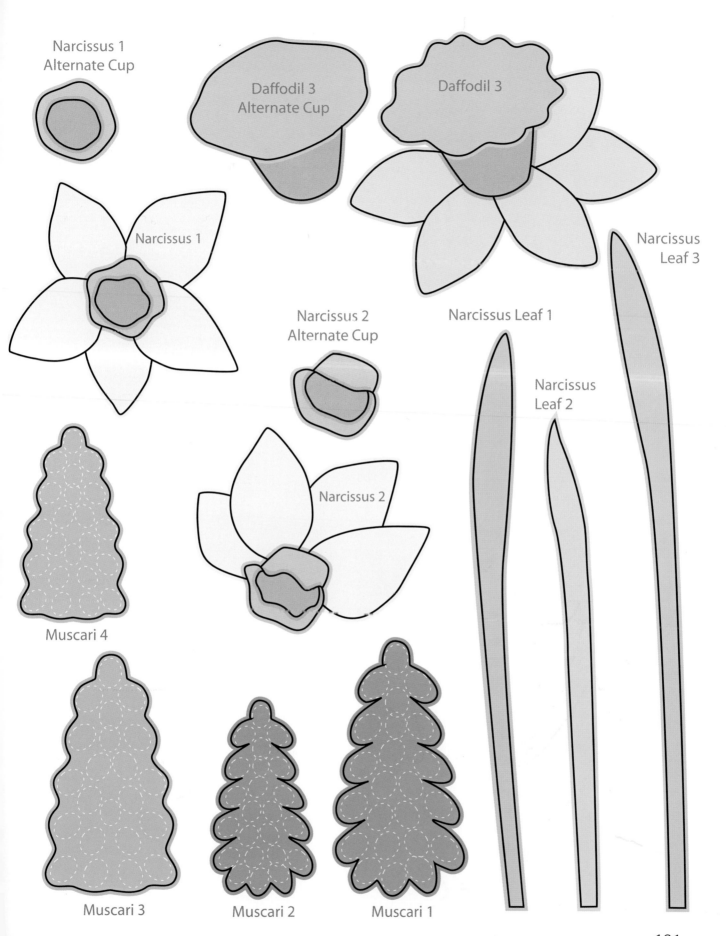

Narcissus 1
Alternate Cup

Daffodil 3
Alternate Cup

Daffodil 3

Narcissus 1

Narcissus
Leaf 3

Narcissus 2
Alternate Cup

Narcissus Leaf 1

Narcissus
Leaf 2

Narcissus 2

Muscari 4

Muscari 3

Muscari 2

Muscari 1

tulips

Pattern Preparation: The tulip (3) was prepared with paper-backed fusible web, page 24.

Stitching: Using rayon thread, stitch the leaf and stem edges with fine zigzag stitches, page 50. Free-motion straight stitch the lower edges of the petals and the leaf veins.

Embellishing: Stitch the upper petal edges with a programmed scroll stitch, page 64.

Copy at 300% for full-size layout

Pattern Preparation: The tulip (3) was prepared with paper-backed fusible web, page 24.

Stitching: Using rayon thread, stitch the lower edges of the petals with fine zigzag stitches, page 50.

Embellishing: Free-motion zigzag stitch the upper edges of the petals, using different shades of thread for some petals, page 66.

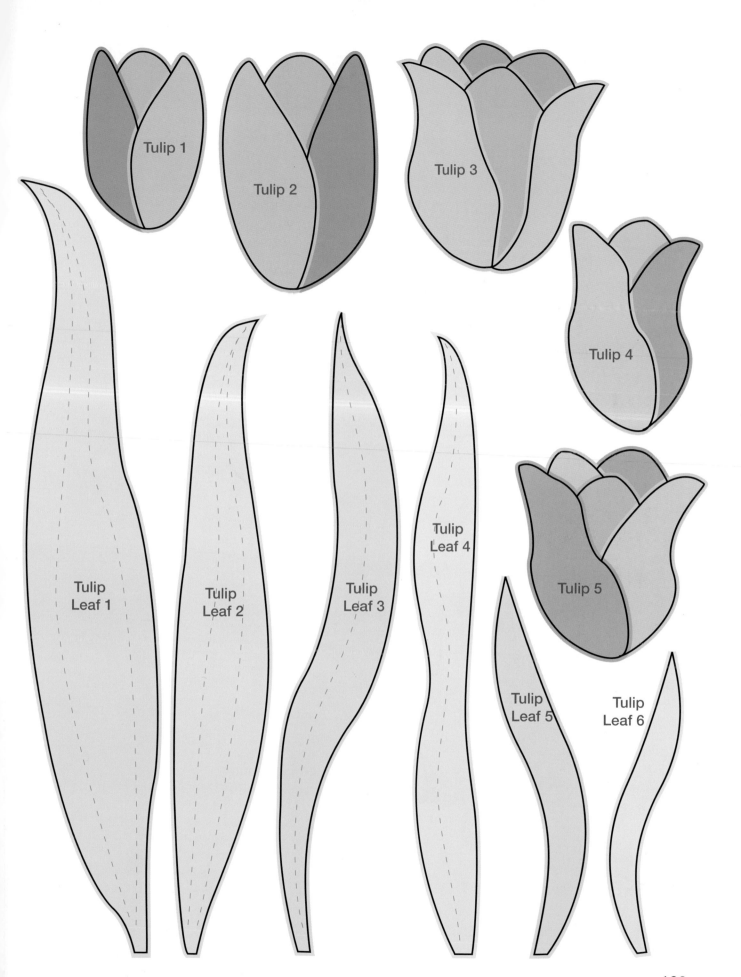

Tulip 1

Tulip 2

Tulip 3

Tulip 4

Tulip 5

Tulip
Leaf 1

Tulip
Leaf 2

Tulip
Leaf 3

Tulip
Leaf 4

Tulip
Leaf 5

Tulip
Leaf 6

hearts and flowers

Mix and match these flower parts to make your own funky flowers.

Pattern Preparation: These hearts (A and C) were prepared with paper-backed fusible web, page 24.

Stitching: Using variegated 30-wt. cotton thread, machine blanket stitch around the large hearts, page 54. Stitch a fine zigzag stitch around the small hearts, page 50.

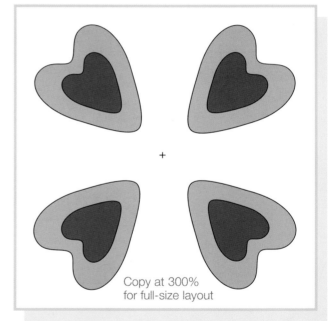

Copy at 300% for full-size layout

Pattern Preparation: The funky flower was prepared with paper-backed fusible web, page 24.

Stitching: Using rayon thread, fine zigzag stitch around the center star and stem, page 50.

Embellishing: Free-motion straight stitch the edges of the petals changing to free-motion circles at the top, page 70. Free-motion straight stitch the edges of the leaves and an echo line about ¼" inside the edge.

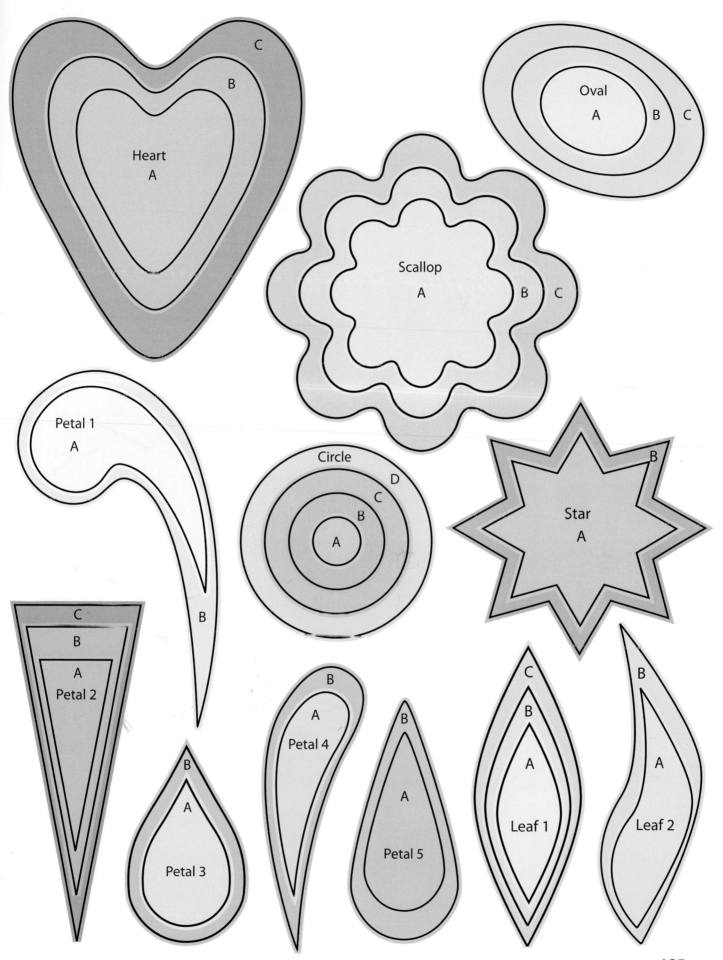

Heart
A
B
C

Oval
A
B
C

Scallop
A
B
C

Petal 1
A
B

Circle
A
B
C
D

Star
A
B

Petal 2
A
B
C

Petal 3
A
B

Petal 4
A
B

Petal 5
A
B

Leaf 1
A
B
C

Leaf 2
A
B

135

roses and star flowers

Pattern Preparation: The rose was prepared with paper-backed fusible web, page 24.

Embellishing: Using rayon thread, satin zigzag stitch the edges of the rose petals, page 65. Increase the stitch width on the outer edges of the petals. Use free-motion straight stitching to make the center detail.

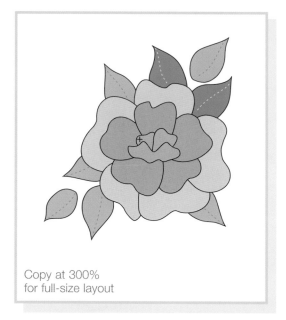

Copy at 300% for full-size layout

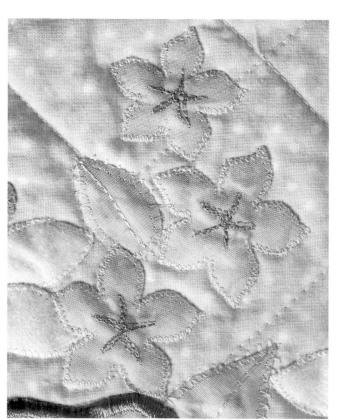

Pattern Preparation: The star flowers were prepared with paper-backed fusible web, page 24.

Stitching: Using matching rayon thread, fine zigzag stitch the edges of the flowers, page 50.

Embellishing: Using a golden color of thread, free-motion straight stitch the five center lines, page 70.

Rose Leaf 1

Rose Leaf 2

Rose Leaf 3

Rose 2

Rose 1

Star Petal 1

Star Petal 2

Star Flower 1

Star Flower 2

137

iris

Pattern Preparation: The iris and leaves were prepared with turned edges.

Stitching: Stitch the edges with invisible blind hem stitch using monofilament invisible thread, page 56.

Embellishing: Using embroidery floss, hand backstitch the veins in the upper petals and long stitch the beard, page 76.

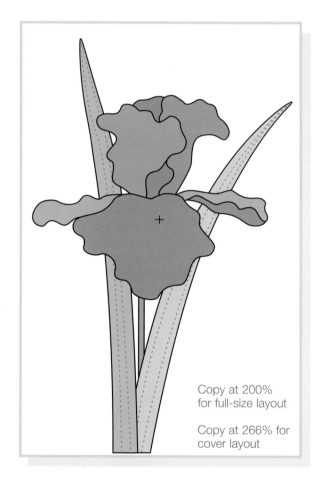

Copy at 200% for full-size layout

Copy at 266% for cover layout

Pattern Preparation: The iris and leaves were prepared with paper-backed fusible web, page 24.

Stitching: Fine zigzag stitch the edges of the leaves and straight stitch the veins, page 68.

Embellishing: Using rayon thread, free-motion zigzag stitch the petals and the beard. Blend shades of yellow and blue on the lower petals, page 66.

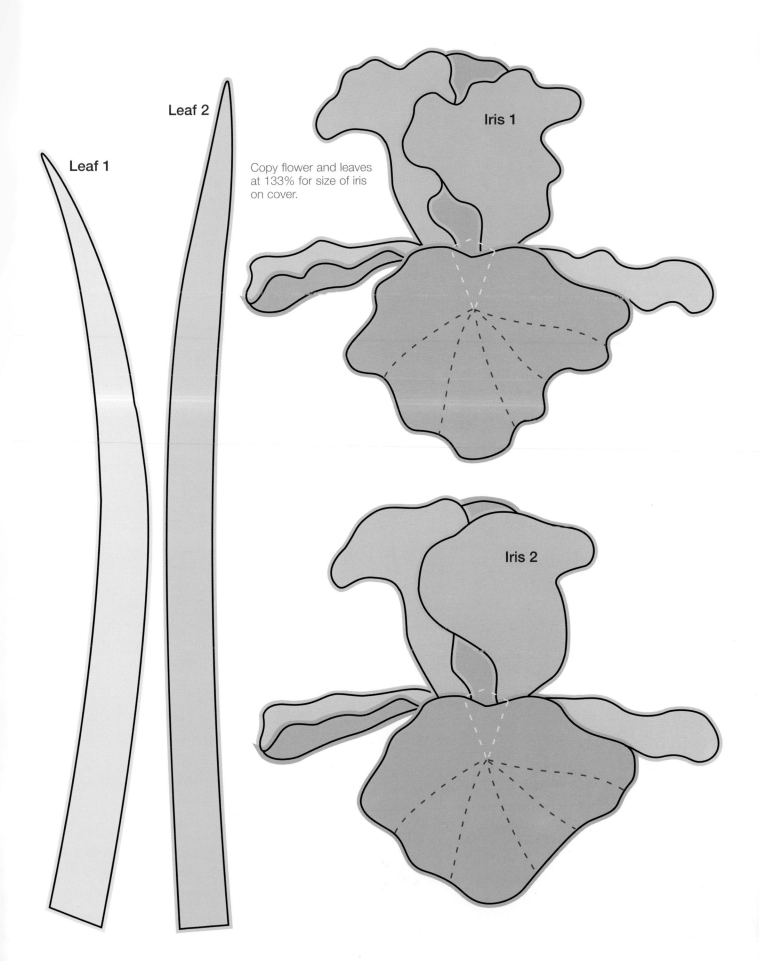

Leaf 1

Leaf 2

Copy flower and leaves
at 133% for size of iris
on cover.

Iris 1

Iris 2

tiger lily

Pattern Preparation: The tiger lily and leaves were prepared with paper-backed fusible web, page 24.

Stitching: Using matching thread, free-motion straight stitch the edges of the leaves and stems, and the veins of the leaves, page 70.

Embellishing: Free-motion zigzag stitch the edges of the petals. Accent the pistil and stamens with beads. For more embellishing details see page 77.

Copy at 300% for full-size layout

Pattern Preparation: The tiger lily and leaves were prepared with paper-backed fusible web, page 24.

Stitching: Using matching thread, free-motion straight stitch the edges of the leaves and stems, and the veins of the leaves, page 70.

Embellishing: Free-motion zigzag stitch the edges of the petals. Accent the pistil and stamens with beads. For more embellishing details see page 77.

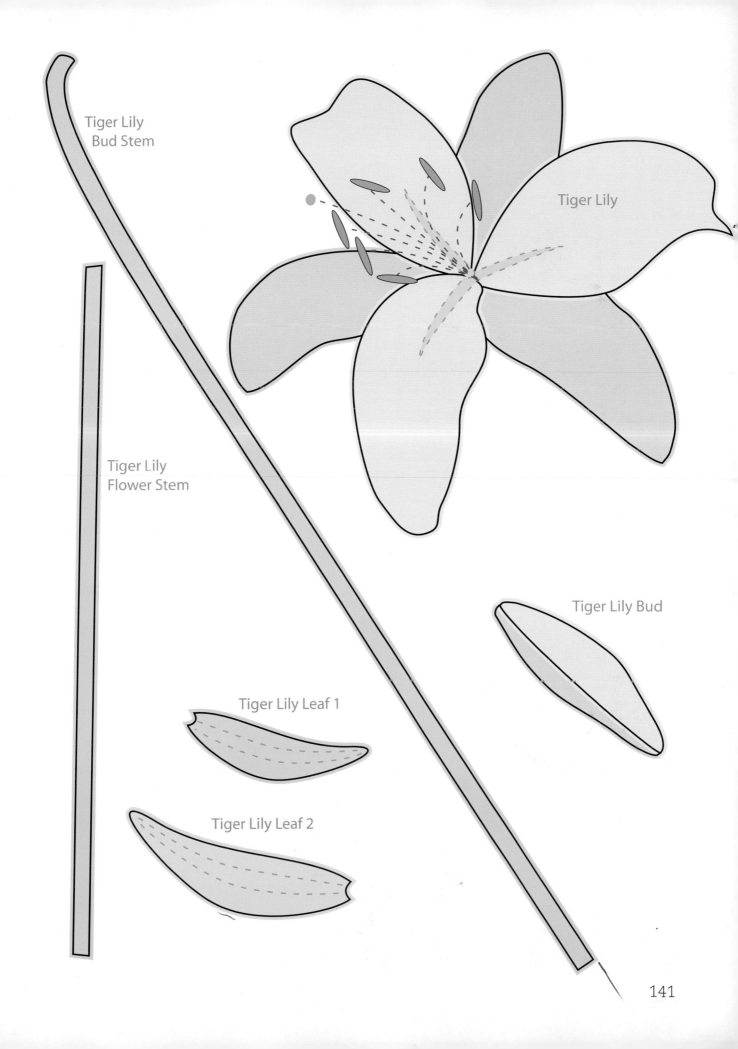

Tiger Lily
Bud Stem

Tiger Lily

Tiger Lily
Flower Stem

Tiger Lily Bud

Tiger Lily Leaf 1

Tiger Lily Leaf 2

index

notebooks

tips

projects

about the author

Janet Pittman

Janet Pittman is an author, designer, editor, teacher, and art quilter. Above all, she sees herself as a graphic designer. All her adult life, she has been designing—clothing, food photographs, quilts.

Janet grew up in Modesto, California. Her father and mother both were graphic designers long before that job description existed, her dad owning a sign shop and painting in watercolor and oils as a hobby, and her mother becoming quite expert in designing and making first pottery, then copper and silver jewelry. Janet recalls her studying *New Yorker* magazine jewelry ads for ideas. And she did needlework; Janet learned sewing, knitting, and embroidery from her mother and grandmother.

"There was good art and there were good crafts going on around me all the time," Janet recalls, and whether the motivation has been environmental or genetic, she has spent her entire adult life in graphic design of one sort or another. She earned a home economics degree at the University of California at Davis, with an emphasis in design and clothing. (She still pursues this interest, designing authentic patterns for Native American and pre-Civil War "mountain man" clothing, for Eagle's View Publishing.)

For Janet, using one skill has led to developing the next. Her post-college job in quality control for a frozen-pie company led to her working in a corporate test kitchen. One of her duties there was setting up—"styling"—food for photography, and she realized she had the gifts necessary for food styling. Her next career move was to Meredith Corporation, *Better Homes and Gardens®*, photo studio, where food for magazine and book illustrations is photographed. Janet says, "I prepared, arranged, and styled the food."

"I really haven't changed much about what I do, just the medium," she says. "Preparation and styling of food for photographs is graphic design with food; quilting and pattern design are graphic design with fabric."

But other design themes were playing too. Janet had been quilting for several years, beginning when she needed something for the blank walls of a new home and took a quilting class. (She never finished that first quilt; she says it is one of her UFOs, "un-finished objects"). She had also been developing a flower garden. After she left her full-time job 10 years ago, these two interests came together when a local advertising firm commissioned her to make king-size quilts to serve as "walls" between office areas.

The firm's clients included agriculture-related businesses, so one of these quilts featured what she terms "giant vignettes of farm animals, vegetables (including a 4 foot ear of corn) sunflowers and so on." After she completed this commission, Janet went into quilting as a business, basing many of her design themes on that "ag" quilt.

Janet explains how she began to add embellishing to her appliqué designs. "After purchasing a new sewing machine 12 years ago, I experimented with different threads and stitches trying to find combinations to enhance the flowers from my garden." From that experimentation comes the look of the quilts she has designed for this book.

Janet lives in West Des Moines, Iowa. She has been designing quilts for 20 years. Her quilts have won several awards and have appeared in *Love of Quilting, American Patchwork & Quilting,* and *Country Marketplace* magazines, and in the Landauer book, *Best-Loved Designers: Quick-Sew Quilts.*

In 1998 she started publishing quilt patterns under the name Garden Trellis Designs, specializing in machine appliqué floral quilts and children's quilts. Contact her at www.gardentrellisdesigns.com.